Tappan's

CW00702477

And Other St

Zane Grey

Alpha Editions

This edition published in 2023

ISBN : 9789357922548

Design and Setting By
Alpha Editions
www.alphaedis.com
Email - info@alphaedis.com

Contents

Tappan's Burro

I

TAPPAN gazed down upon the newly-born little burro with something of pity and consternation. It was not a vigorous offspring of the redoubtable Jennie, champion of all the numberless burros he had driven in his desert-prospecting years. He could not leave it there to die. Surely it was not strong enough to follow its mother. And to kill it was beyond him.

"Poor little devil!" soliloquized Tappan. "Reckon neither Jennie nor I wanted it to be born.... I'll have to hold up in this camp a few days. You can never tell what a burro will do. It might fool us an' grow strong all of a sudden."

Whereupon Tappan left Jennie and her tiny, gray lop-eared baby to themselves, and leisurely set about making permanent camp. The water at this oasis was not much to his liking, but it was drinkable, and he felt he must put up with it. For the rest the oasis was desirable enough as a camping site. Desert wanderers like Tappan favored the lonely water holes. This one was up under the bold brow of the Chocolate Mountains, where rocky wall met the desert sand, and a green patch of *palo verdes* and mesquites proved the presence of water. It had a magnificent view down a many-leagued slope of desert growths, across the dark belt of green and the shining strip of red that marked the Rio Colorado, and on to the upflung Arizona land, range lifting to range until the saw-toothed peaks notched the blue sky.

Locked in the iron fastnesses of these desert mountains was gold. Tappan, if he had any calling, was a prospector. But the lure of gold did not bind him to this wandering life any more than the freedom of it. He had never made a rich strike. About the best he could ever do was to dig enough gold to grubstake himself for another prospecting trip into some remote corner of the American Desert. Tappan knew the arid Southwest from San Diego to the Pecos River and from Picacho on the Colorado to the Tonto Basin. Few prospectors had the strength and endurance of Tappan. He was a giant in build, and at thirty-five had never yet reached the limit of his physical force.

With hammer and pick and magnifying glass Tappan scaled the bare ridges. He was not an expert in testing minerals. He knew he might easily pass by a rich vein of ore. But he did his best, sure at least that no prospector could get more than he out of the pursuit of gold. Tappan was more of a naturalist than a prospector, and more of a dreamer than either. Many were the idle moments that he sat staring down the vast reaches of the valleys, or watching some creature of the wasteland, or marveling at the vivid hues of desert flowers.

Tappan waited two weeks at this oasis for Jennie's baby burro to grow strong enough to walk. And the very day that Tappan decided to break camp he found signs of gold at the head of a wash above the oasis. Quite by chance, as he was looking for his burros, he struck his pick into a place no different from a thousand others there, and hit into a pocket of gold. He cleaned out the pocket before sunset, the richer for several thousand dollars.

"You brought me luck," said Tappan, to the little gray burro staggering round its mother. "Your name is Jenet. You're Tappan's burro, an' I reckon he'll stick to you."

Jenet belied the promise of her birth. Like a weed in fertile ground she grew. Winter and summer Tappan patroled the sand beats from one trading post to another, and his burros traveled with him. Jenet had an especially good training. Her mother had happened to be a remarkably good burro before Tappan had bought her. And Tappan had patience; he found leisure to do things, and he had something of pride in Jenet. Whenever he happened to drop into Ehrenberg or Yuma, or any freighting station, some prospector always tried to buy Jenet. She grew as large as a medium-sized mule, and a three-hundred-pound pack was no load to discommode her.

Tappan, in common with most lonely wanderers of the desert, talked to his burro. As the years passed this habit grew, until Tappan would talk to Jenet just to hear the sound of his voice. Perhaps that was all which kept him human.

"Jenet, you're worthy of a happier life," Tappan would say, as he unpacked her after a long day's march over the barren land. "You're a ship of the desert. Here we are, with grub an' water, a hundred miles from any camp. An' what but you could have fetched me here? No horse! No mule! No man! Nothin' but a camel, an' so I call you ship of the desert. But for you an' your kind, Jenet, there'd be no prospectors, and few gold mines. Reckon the desert would be still an unknown waste.... You're a great beast of burden, Jenet, an' there's no one to sing your praise."

And of a golden sunrise, when Jenet was packed and ready to face the cool, sweet fragrance of the desert, Tappan was wont to say:

"Go along with you, Jenet. The mornin's fine. Look at the mountains yonder callin' us. It's only a step down there. All purple an' violet! It's the life for us, my burro, an' Tappan's as rich as if all these sands were pearls."

But sometimes, at sunset, when the way had been long and hot and rough, Tappan would bend his shaggy head over Jenet, and talk in different mood. "Another day gone, Jenet, another journey ended—an' Tappan is only older, wearier, sicker. There's no reward for your faithfulness. I'm only a desert rat, livin' from hole to hole. No home! No face to see.... Some sunset, Jenet, we'll reach the end of the trail. An' Tappan's bones will bleach in the sands. An' no one will know or care!"

When Jenet was two years old she would have taken the blue ribbon in competition with all the burros of the Southwest. She was unusually large and strong, perfectly proportioned, sound in every particular, and practically tireless. But these were not the only characteristics that made prospectors envious of Tappan. Jenet had the common virtues of all good burros magnified to an unbelievable degree. Moreover, she had sense and instinct that to Tappan bordered on the supernatural.

During these years Tappan's trail crisscrossed the mineral region of the Southwest. But, as always, the rich strike held aloof. It was like the pot of gold buried at the foot of the rainbow. Jenet knew the trails and the water holes better than Tappan. She could follow a trail obliterated by drifting sand or cut out by running water. She could scent at long distance a new spring on the desert or a strange water hole. She never wandered far from camp so that Tappan had to walk far in search of her. Wild burros, the bane of most prospectors, held no charm for Jenet. And she had never yet shown any especial liking for a tame burro. This was the strangest feature of Jenet's complex character. Burros were noted for their habit of pairing off, and forming friendships for one or more comrades. These relations were permanent. But Jenet still remained fancy free.

Tappan scarcely realized how he relied upon this big, gray, serene beast of burden. Of course, when chance threw him among men of his calling he would brag about her. But he had never really appreciated Jenet. In his way Tappan was a brooding, plodding fellow, not conscious of sentiment. When he bragged about Jenet it was her good qualities upon which he dilated. But what he really liked best about her were the little things of every day.

During the earlier years of her training Jenet had been a thief. She would pretend to be asleep for hours just to get a chance to steal something out of camp. Tappan had broken this habit in its incipiency. But he never quite trusted her. Jenet was a burro.

Jenet ate anything offered her. She could fare for herself or go without. Whatever Tappan had left from his own meals was certain to be rich dessert for Jenet. Every meal time she would stand near the camp fire, with one great

- 3 -

long ear drooping, and the other standing erect. Her expression was one of meekness, of unending patience. She would lick a tin can until it shone resplendent. On long, hard, barren trails Jenet's deportment did not vary from that where the water holes and grassy patches were many. She did not need to have grass or grain. Brittle-bush and sage were good fare for her. She could eat greasewood, a desert plant that protected itself with a sap as sticky as varnish and far more dangerous to animals. She could eat cacti. Tappan had seen her break off leaves of the prickly pear cactus, and stamp upon them with her forefeet, mashing off the thorns, so that she could consume the succulent pulp. She liked mesquite beans, and leaves of willow, and all the trailing vines of the desert. And she could subsist in an arid waste land where a man would have died in short order.

No ascent or descent was too hard or dangerous for Jenet, provided it was possible of accomplishment. She would refuse a trail that was impassable. She seemed to have an uncanny instinct both for what she could do, and what was beyond a burro. Tappan had never known her to fail on something to which she stuck persistently. Swift streams of water, always bugbears to burros, did not stop Jenet. She hated quicksand, but could be trusted to navigate it, if that were possible. When she stepped gingerly, with little inch steps, out upon thin crust of ice or salty crust of desert sink hole, Tappan would know that it was safe, or she would turn back. Thunder and lightning, intense heat or bitter cold, the sirocco sand storm of the desert, the white dust of the alkali wastes—these were all the same to Jenet.

One August, the hottest and driest of his desert experience, Tappan found himself working a most promising claim in the lower reaches of the Panamint Mountains on the northern slope above Death Valley. It was a hard country at the most favorable season; in August it was terrible.

The Panamints were infested by various small gangs of desperadoes—outlaw claim jumpers where opportunity afforded—and out-and-out robbers, even murderers where they could not get the gold any other way.

Tappan had been warned not to go into this region alone. But he never heeded any warnings. And the idea that he would ever strike a claim or dig enough gold to make himself an attractive target for outlaws seemed preposterous and not worth considering. Tappan had become a wanderer now from the unbreakable habit of it. Much to his amaze he struck a rich ledge of free gold in a canyon of the Panamints; and he worked from daylight until dark. He forgot about the claim jumpers, until one day he saw Jenet's long ears go up in the manner habitual with her when she saw strange men. Tappan watched the rest of that day, but did not catch a glimpse of any living thing. It was a desolate place, shut in, red-walled, hazy with heat, and brooding with an eternal silence.

Not long after that Tappan discovered boot tracks of several men adjacent to his camp and in an out-of-the-way spot, which persuaded him that he was being watched. Claim jumpers who were not going to jump his claim in this torrid heat, but meant to let him dig the gold and then kill him. Tappan was not the kind of man to be afraid. He grew wrathful and stubborn. He had six small canvas bags of gold and did not mean to lose them. Still, he was worried.

"Now, what's best to do?" he pondered. "I mustn't give it away that I'm wise. Reckon I'd better act natural. But I can't stay here longer. My claim's about worked out. An' these jumpers are smart enough to know it.... I've got to make a break at night. What to do?"

Tappan did not want to cache the gold, for in that case, of course, he would have to return for it. Still, he reluctantly admitted to himself that this was the best way to save it. Probably these robbers were watching him day and night. It would be most unwise to attempt escaping by traveling up over the Panamints.

"Reckon my only chance is goin' down into Death Valley," soliloquized Tappan, grimly.

The alternative thus presented was not to his liking. Crossing Death Valley at this season was always perilous, and never attempted in the heat of day. And at this particular time of intense torridity, when the day heat was unendurable and the midnight furnace gales were blowing, it was an enterprise from which even Tappan shrank. Added to this were the facts that he was too far west of the narrow part of the valley, and even if he did get across he would find himself in the most forbidding and desolate region of the Funeral Mountains.

Thus thinking and planning, Tappan went about his mining and camp tasks, trying his best to act natural. But he did not succeed. It was impossible, while expecting a shot at any moment, to act as if there was nothing on his mind. His camp lay at the bottom of a rocky slope. A tiny spring of water made verdure of grass and mesquite, welcome green in all that stark iron nakedness. His camp site was out in the open, on the bench near the spring. The gold claim that Tappan was working was not visible from any vantage point either below or above. It lay back at the head of a break in the rocky wall. It had two virtues—one that the sun never got to it, and the other that it was well hidden. Once there, Tappan knew he could not be seen. This, however, did not diminish his growing uneasiness. The solemn stillness was a menace. The heat of the day appeared to be augmenting to a degree beyond his experience.

Every few moments Tappan would slip back through a narrow defile in the rocks and peep from his covert down at the camp. On the last of these occasions he saw Jenet out in the open. She stood motionless. Her long ears were erect. In an instant Tappan became strung with thrilling excitement. His keen eyes searched every approach to his camp. And at last in the gully below to the right he discovered two men crawling along from rock to rock. Jenet had seen them enter that gully and was now watching for them to appear.

Tappan's excitement gave place to a grimmer emotion. These stealthy visitors were going to hide in ambush, and kill him as he returned to camp.

"Jenet, reckon what I owe you is a whole lot," muttered Tappan. "They'd have got me sure.... But now—"

Tappan left his tools, and crawled out of his covert into the jumble of huge rocks toward the left of the slope. He had a six-shooter. His rifle he had left in camp. Tappan had seen only two men, but he knew there were more than that, if not actually near at hand at the moment, then surely not far away. And his chance was to worm his way like an Indian down to camp. With the rifle in his possession he would make short work of the present difficulty.

"Lucky Jenet's right in camp!" said Tappan, to himself. "It beats hell how she does things!"

Tappan was already deciding to pack and hurry away. On the moment Death Valley did not daunt him. This matter of crawling and gliding along was work unsuited to his great stature. He was too big to hide behind a little shrub or a rock. And he was not used to stepping lightly. His hobnailed boots could not be placed noiselessly upon the stones. Moreover, he could not progress without displacing little bits of weathered rock. He was sure that keen ears not too far distant could have heard him. But he kept on, making good progress around that slope to the far side of the canyon. Fortunately, he headed the gully up which his ambushers were stealing. On the other hand, this far side of the canyon afforded but little cover. The sun had gone down back of the huge red mass of the mountain. It had left the rocks so hot Tappan could not touch them with his bare hands.

He was about to stride out from his last covert and make a run for it down the rest of the slope, when, surveying the whole amphitheater below him, he espied the two men coming up out of the gully, headed toward his camp. They looked in his direction. Surely they had heard or seen him. But Tappan perceived at a glance that he was the closer to the camp. Without another moment of hesitation, he plunged from his hiding place, down the weathered slope. His giant strides set the loose rocks sliding and rattling. The men saw him. The foremost yelled to the one behind him. Then they both broke into a run. Tappan reached the level of the bench, and saw he could beat either of them into the camp. Unless he were disabled! He felt the wind of a heavy bullet before he heard it strike the rocks beyond. Then followed the boom of a Colt. One of his enemies had halted to shoot. This spurred Tappan to tremendous exertion. He flew over the rough ground, scarcely hearing the rapid shots. He could no longer see the man who was firing. But the first one was in plain sight, running hard, not yet seeing he was out of the race.

When he became aware of that he halted, and dropping on one knee, leveled his gun at the running Tappan. The distance was scarcely sixty yards. His first shot did not allow for Tappan's speed. His second kicked up the gravel in Tappan's face. Then followed three more shots in rapid succession. The man divined that Tappan had a rifle in camp. Then he steadied himself, waiting for the moment when Tappan had to slow down and halt. As Tappan reached his camp and dove for his rifle, the robber took time for his last aim, evidently hoping to get a stationary target. But Tappan did not get up from behind his camp duffel. It had been a habit of his to pile his boxes of supplies and roll of bedding together, and cover them with a canvas. He poked his rifle over the top of this and shot the robber.

Then, leaping up, he ran forward to get sight of the second one. This man began to run along the edge of the gully. Tappan fired rapidly at him. The third shot knocked the fellow down. But he got up, and yelling, as if for succor, he ran off. Tappan got another shot before he disappeared.

"Ahuh!" grunted Tappan, grimly. His keen gaze came back to survey the fallen robber, and then went out over the bench, across the wide mouth of the canyon. Tappan thought he had better utilize time to pack instead of pursuing the fleeing man.

Reloading the rifle, he hurried out to find Jenet. She was coming in to camp.

"Shore you're a treasure, old girl!" ejaculated Tappan.

Never in his life had he packed Jenet, or any other burro, so quickly. His last act was to drink all he could hold, fill his two canteens, and make Jenet drink. Then, rifle in hand, he drove the burro out of camp, round the corner of the red wall, to the wide gateway that opened down into Death Valley.

Tappan looked back more than he looked ahead. And he had traveled down a mile or more before he began to breathe more easily. He had escaped the claim jumpers. Even if they did show up in pursuit now, they could never catch him. Tappan believed he could travel faster and farther than any men of that ilk. But they did not appear. Perhaps the crippled one had not been able to reach his comrades in time. More likely, however, the gang had no taste for a chase in that torrid heat.

Tappan slowed his stride. He was almost as wet with sweat as if he had fallen into the spring. The great beads rolled down his face. And there seemed to be little streams of fire trickling down his breast. But despite this, and his labored panting for breath, not until he halted in the shade of a rocky wall did he realize the heat.

It was terrific. Instantly then he knew he was safe from pursuit. But he knew also that he faced a greater peril than that of robbers. He could fight evil men, but he could not fight this heat.

So he rested there, regaining his breath. Already thirst was acute. Jenet stood near by, watching him. Tappan, with his habit of humanizing the burro, imagined that Jenet looked serious. A moment's thought was enough for Tappan to appreciate the gravity of his situation. He was about to go down into the upper end of Death Valley—a part of that country unfamiliar to him. He must cross it, and also the Funeral Mountains, at a season when a prospector who knew the trails and water holes would have to be forced to undertake it. Tappan had no choice.

His rifle was too hot to hold, so he stuck it in Jenet's pack; and, burdened only by a canteen of water, he set out, driving the burro ahead. Once he looked back up the wide-mouthed canyon. It appeared to smoke with red heat veils. The silence was oppressive.

Presently he turned the last corner that obstructed sight of Death Valley. Tappan had never been appalled by any aspect of the desert, but it was certain that here he halted. Back in his mountain-walled camp the sun had passed behind the high domes, but here it still held most of the valley in its blazing grip. Death Valley looked a ghastly, glaring level of white, over which a strange dull leaden haze drooped like a blanket. Ghosts of mountain peaks appeared to show dim and vague. There was no movement of anything. No wind! The valley was dead. Desolation reigned supreme. Tappan could not see far toward either end of the valley. A few miles of white glare merged at last into leaden pall. A strong odor, not unlike sulphur, seemed to add weight to the air.

Tappan strode on, mindful that Jenet had decided opinions of her own. She did not want to go straight ahead or to right or left, but back. That was the one direction impossible for Tappan. And he had to resort to a rare measure—that of beating her. But at last Jenet accepted the inevitable and headed down into the stark and naked plain. Soon Tappan reached the margin of the zone of shade cast by the mountain and was now exposed to the sun. The difference seemed tremendous. He had been hot, oppressed, weighted. It was now as if he was burned through his clothes, and walked on red-hot sands.

When Tappan ceased to sweat and his skin became dry, he drank half a canteen of water, and slowed his stride. Inured to desert hardship as he was, he could not long stand this. Jenet did not exhibit any lessening of vigor. In truth what she showed now was an increasing nervousness. It was almost as if she scented an enemy. Tappan never before had such faith in her. Jenet was equal to this task.

With that blazing sun on his back, Tappan felt he was being pursued by a furnace. He was compelled to drink the remaining half of his first canteen of water. Sunset would save him. Two more hours of such insupportable heat would lay him prostrate.

The ghastly glare of the valley took on a reddish tinge. The heat was blinding Tappan. The time came when he walked beside Jenet with a hand on her pack, for his eyes could no longer endure the furnace glare. Even with them closed he knew when the sun sank behind the Panamints. That fire no longer followed him. And the red left his eyelids.

With the sinking of the sun the world of Death Valley changed. It smoked with heat veils. But the intolerable constant burn was gone. The change was so immense that it seemed to have brought coolness.

In the twilight—strange, ghostly, somber, silent as death—Tappan followed Jenet off the sand, down upon the silt and borax level, to the crusty salt. Before dark Jenet halted at a sluggish belt of fluid—acid, it appeared to Tappan. It was not deep. And the bottom felt stable. But Jenet refused to cross. Tappan trusted her judgment more than his own. Jenet headed to the left and followed the course of the strange stream.

Night intervened. A night without stars or sky or sound, hot, breathless, charged with some intangible current! Tappan dreaded the midnight furnace winds of Death Valley. He had never encountered them. He had heard prospectors say that any man caught in Death Valley when these gales blew would never get out to tell the tale. And Jenet seemed to have something on her mind. She was no longer a leisurely, complacent burro. Tappan imagined Jenet seemed stern. Most assuredly she knew now which way she wanted to travel. It was not easy for Tappan to keep up with her, and ten paces beyond him she was out of sight.

At last Jenet headed the acid wash, and turned across the valley into a field of broken salt crust, like the roughened ice of a river that had broken and jammed, then frozen again. Impossible was it to make even a reasonable headway. It was a zone, however, that eventually gave way to Jenet's instinct for direction. Tappan had long ceased to try to keep his bearings. North, south, east, and west were all the same to him. The night was a blank—the darkness a wall—the silence a terrible menace flung at any living creature.

Death Valley had endured them millions of years before living creatures had existed. It was no place for a man.

Tappan was now three hundred and more feet below sea level, in the aftermath of a day that had registered one hundred and forty-five degrees of heat. He knew, when he began to lose thought and balance—when only the primitive instincts directed his bodily machine. And he struggled with all his will power to keep hold of his sense of sight and feeling. He hoped to cross the lower level before the midnight gales began to blow.

Tappan's hope was vain. According to record, once in a long season of intense heat, there came a night when the furnace winds broke their schedule, and began early. The misfortune of Tappan was that he had struck this night.

Suddenly it seemed that the air, sodden with heat, began to move. It had weight. It moved soundlessly and ponderously. But it gathered momentum. Tappan realized what was happening. The blanket of heat generated by the day was yielding to outside pressure. Something had created a movement of the hotter air that must find its way upward, to give place for the cooler air that must find its way down.

Tappan heard the first, low, distant moan of wind and it struck terror to his heart. It did not have an earthly sound. Was that a knell for him? Nothing was surer than the fact that the desert must sooner or later claim him as a victim. Grim and strong, he rebelled against the conviction.

That moan was a forerunner of others, growing louder and longer until the weird sound became continuous. Then the movement of wind was accelerated and began to carry a fine dust. Dark as the night was, it did not hide the pale sheets of dust that moved along the level plain. Tappan's feet felt the slow rise in the floor of the valley. His nose recognized the zone of borax and alkali and niter and sulphur. He had reached the pit of the valley at the time of the furnace winds.

The moan augmented to a roar, coming like a mighty storm through a forest. It was hellish—like the woeful tide of Acheron. It enveloped Tappan. And the gale bore down in tremendous volume, like a furnace blast. Tappan seemed to feel his body penetrated by a million needles of fire. He seemed to dry up. The blackness of night had a spectral, whitish cast; the gloom was a whirling medium; the valley floor was lost in a sheeted, fiercely seeping stream of silt. Deadly fumes swept by, not lingering long enough to suffocate Tappan. He would gasp and choke—then the poison gas was gone on the gale. But hardest to endure was the heavy body of moving heat. Tappan grew blind, so that he had to hold to Jenet, and stumble along. Every gasping breath was a tortured effort. He could not bear a scarf over his face. His lungs heaved like great leather bellows. His heart pumped like an engine short of fuel. This was the supreme test for his never proven endurance. And he was all but vanquished.

Tappan's senses of sight and smell and hearing failed him. There was left only the sense of touch—a feeling of rope and burro and ground—and an awful insulating pressure upon all his body. His feet marked a change from salty plain to sandy ascent and then to rocky slope. The pressure of wind gradually lessened: the difference in air made life possible; the feeling of being dragged endlessly by Jenet had ceased. Tappan went his limit and fell into oblivion.

When he came to, he was suffering bodily tortures. Sight was dim. But he saw walls of rocks, green growths of mesquite, tamarack, and grass. Jenet was lying down, with her pack flopped to one side. Tappan's dead ears recovered to a strange murmuring, babbling sound. Then he realized his deliverance. Jenet had led him across Death Valley, up into the mountain range, straight to a spring of running water.

THIS WAS THE SUPREME TEST FOR HIS NEVER-PROVEN ENDURANCE, AND HE WAS ALL BUT VANQUISHED

Tappan crawled to the edge of the water and drank guardedly, a little at a time. He had to quell terrific craving to drink his fill. Then he crawled to Jenet, and loosening the ropes of her pack, freed her from its burden. Jenet got up, apparently none the worse for her ordeal. She gazed mildly at Tappan, as if to say: "Well, I got you out of that hole."

Tappan returned her gaze. Were they only man and beast, alone in the desert? She seemed magnified to Tappan, no longer a plodding, stupid burro.

"Jenet, you—saved—my life," Tappan tried to enunciate. "I'll never—forget."

Tappan was struck then to a realization of Jenet's service. He was unutterably grateful. Yet the time came when he did forget.

II

TAPPAN had a weakness common to all prospectors: Any tale of a lost gold mine would excite his interest; and well-known legends of lost mines always obsessed him.

Peg-leg Smith's lost gold mine had lured Tappan to no less than half a dozen trips into the terrible shifting-sand country of southern California. There was no water near the region said to hide this mine of fabulous wealth. Many prospectors had left their bones to bleach white in the sun, finally to be buried by the ever blowing sands. Upon the occasion of Tappan's last escape from this desolate and forbidding desert, he had promised Jenet never to undertake it again. It seemed Tappan promised the faithful burro a good many things. It had been a habit.

When Tappan had a particularly hard experience or perilous adventure, he always took a dislike to the immediate country where it had befallen him. Jenet had dragged him across Death Valley, through incredible heat and the midnight furnace winds of that strange place; and he had promised her he would never forget how she had saved his life. Nor would he ever go back to Death Valley! He made his way over the Funeral Mountains, worked down through Nevada, and crossed the Rio Colorado above Needles, and entered Arizona. He traveled leisurely, but he kept going, and headed southeast towards Globe. There he cashed one of his six bags of gold, and indulged in the luxury of a complete new outfit. Even Jenet appreciated this fact, for the old outfit would scarcely hold together.

Tappan had the other five bags of gold in his pack; and after hours of hesitation he decided he would not cash them and entrust the money to a bank. He would take care of them. For him the value of this gold amounted to a small fortune. Many plans suggested themselves to Tappan. But in the end he grew weary of them. What did he want with a ranch, or cattle, or an outfitting store, or any of the businesses he now had the means to buy? Towns soon palled on Tappan. People did not long please him. Selfish interest and greed seemed paramount everywhere. Besides, if he acquired a place to take up his time, what would become of Jenet? That question decided him. He packed the burro and once more took to the trails.

A dim, lofty, purple range called alluringly to Tappan. The Superstition Mountains! Somewhere in that purple mass hid the famous treasure called the Lost Dutchman gold mine. Tappan had heard the story often. A Dutch prospector struck gold in the Superstitions. He kept the location secret. When he ran short of money, he would disappear for a few weeks, and then return with bags of gold. Wherever his strike, it assuredly was a rich one. No one ever could trail him or get a word out of him. Time passed. A few years made him old. During this time he conceived a liking for a young man, and eventually confided to him that some day he would tell him the secret of his gold mine. He had drawn a map of the landmarks adjacent to his mine. But he was careful not to put on paper directions how to get there. It chanced that he suddenly fell ill and saw his end was near. Then he summoned the young man who had been so fortunate as to win his regard. Now this individual was a ne'er-do-well, and upon this occasion he was half drunk. The dying Dutchman produced his map, and gave it with verbal directions to the young man. Then he died. When the recipient of this fortune recovered from the effects of liquor, he could not remember all the Dutchman had told him. He tortured himself to remember names and places. But the mine was up in the Superstition Mountains. He never remembered. He never found the lost mine, though he spent his life and died trying. Thus the story passed into the legend of the Lost Dutchman.

Tappan now had his try at finding it. But for him the shifting sands of the southern California desert or even the barren and desolate Death Valley were preferable to this Superstition Range. It was a harder country than the Pinacate of Sonora. Tappan hated cactus, and the Superstitions were full of it. Everywhere stood up the huge *sahuaro*, the giant cacti of the Arizona plateaus, tall like branchless trees, fluted and columnar, beautiful and fascinating to gaze upon, but obnoxious to prospector and burro.

One day from a north slope Tappan saw afar a wonderful country of black timber, above which zigzagged for many miles a yellow, winding rampart of rock. This he took to be the rim of the Mogollon Mesa, one of Arizona's freaks of nature. Something called Tappan. He was forever victim to yearnings for the unattainable. He was tired of heat, glare, dust, bare rock, and thorny cactus. The Lost Dutchman gold mine was a myth. Besides, he did not need any more gold.

Next morning Tappan packed Jenet and worked down off the north slopes of the Superstition Range. That night about sunset he made camp on the bank of a clear brook, with grass and wood in abundance—such a camp site as a prospector dreamed of but seldom found.

Before dark Jenet's long ears told of the advent of strangers. A man and a woman rode down the trail into Tappan's camp. They had poor horses, and led a pack animal that appeared too old and weak to bear up under even the meager pack he carried.

"Howdy," said the man.

Tappan rose from his task to his lofty height and returned the greeting. The man was middle-aged, swarthy, and rugged, a mountaineer, with something about him that Tappan instinctively distrusted. The woman was under thirty, comely in a full-blown way, with rich brown skin and glossy dark hair. She had wide-open black eyes that bent a curious possession-taking gaze upon Tappan.

"Care if we camp with you?" she inquired, and she smiled.

That smile changed Tappan's habit and conviction of a lifetime.

"No indeed. Reckon I'd like a little company," he said.

Very probably Jenet did not understand Tappan's words, but she dropped one ear, and walked out of camp to the green bank.

"Thanks, stranger," replied the woman. "That grub shore smells good." She hesitated a moment, evidently waiting to catch her companion's eye, then she continued. "My name's Madge Beam. He's my brother Jake.... Who might you happen to be?"

"I'm Tappan, lone prospector, as you see," replied Tappan.

"Tappan! What's your front handle?" she queried, curiously.

"Fact is, I don't remember," replied Tappan, as he brushed a huge hand through his shaggy hair.

"Ahuh? Any name's good enough."

When she dismounted, Tappan saw that she had a tall, lithe figure, garbed in rider's overalls and boots. She unsaddled her horse with the dexterity of long practice. The saddlebags she carried over to the spot the man Jake had selected to throw the pack.

Tappan heard them talking in low tones. It struck him as strange that he did not have his usual reaction to an invasion of his privacy and solitude. Tappan had thrilled under those black eyes. And now a queer sensation of the unusual rose in him. Bending over his camp-fire tasks he pondered this and that, but mostly the sense of the nearness of a woman. Like most desert men, Tappan knew little of the other sex. A few that he might have been drawn to went out of his wandering life as quickly as they had entered it. This Madge Beam took possession of his thoughts. An evidence of Tappan's preoccupation was the fact that he burned his first batch of biscuits. And Tappan felt proud of his culinary ability. He was on his knees, mixing more flour and water, when the woman spoke from right behind him.

"Tough luck you burned the first pan," she said. "But it's a good turn for your burro. That shore is a burro. Biggest I ever saw."

She picked up the burned biscuits and tossed them over to Jenet. Then she came back to Tappan's side, rather embarrassingly close.

"Tappan, I know how I'll eat, so I ought to ask you to let me help," she said, with a laugh.

"No, I don't need any," replied Tappan. "You sit down on my roll of beddin' there. Must be tired, aren't you?"

"Not so very," she returned. "That is, I'm not tired of ridin'." She spoke the second part of this reply in lower tone.

Tappan looked up from his task. The woman had washed her face, brushed her hair, and had put on a skirt—a singularly attractive change. Tappan thought her younger. She was the handsomest woman he had ever seen. The look of her made him clumsy. What eyes she had! They looked through him. Tappan returned to his task, wondering if he was right in his surmise that she wanted to be friendly.

"Jake an' I drove a bunch of cattle to Maricopa," she volunteered. "We sold 'em, an' Jake gambled away most of the money. I couldn't get what I wanted."

"Too bad! So you're ranchers. Once thought I'd like that. Fact is, down here at Globe a few weeks ago I came near buyin' some rancher out an' tryin' the game."

"You did?" Her query had a low, quick eagerness that somehow thrilled Tappan. But he did not look up.

"I'm a wanderer. I'd never do on a ranch."

"But if you had a woman?" Her laugh was subtle and gay.

"A woman! For me? Oh, Lord, no!" ejaculated Tappan, in confusion.

"Why not? Are you a woman hater?"

"I can't say that," replied Tappan, soberly. "It's just—I guess—no woman would have me."

"Faint heart never won fair lady."

Tappan had no reply for that. He surely was making a mess of the second pan of biscuit dough. Manifestly the woman saw this, for with a laugh she plumped down on her knees in front of Tappan, and rolled her sleeves up over shapely brown arms.

"Poor man! Shore you need a woman. Let me show you," she said, and put her hands right down upon Tappan's. The touch gave him a strange thrill. He had to pull his hands away, and as he wiped them with his scarf he looked at her. He seemed compelled to look. She was close to him now, smiling in good nature, a little scornful of man's encroachment upon the housewifely duties of a woman. A subtle something emanated from her—a more than kindness or gayety. Tappan grasped that it was just the woman of her. And it was going to his head.

"Very well, let's see you show me," he replied, as he rose to his feet.

Just then the brother Jake strolled over, and he had a rather amused and derisive eye for his sister.

"Wal, Tappan, she's not overfond of work, but I reckon she can cook," he said.

Tappan felt greatly relieved at the approach of this brother. And he fell into conversation with him, telling something of his prospecting since leaving Globe, and listening to the man's cattle talk. By and by the woman called, "Come an' get it!" Then they sat down to eat, and, as usual with hungry wayfarers, they did not talk much until appetite was satisfied. Afterward, before the camp fire, they began to talk again, Jake being the most discursive. Tappan conceived the idea that the rancher was rather curious about him, and perhaps wanted to sell his ranch. The woman seemed more thoughtful, with her wide black eyes on the fire.

"Tappan, what way you travelin'?" finally inquired Beam.

"Can't say. I just worked down out of the Superstitions. Haven't any place in mind. Where does this road go?"

"To the Tonto Basin. Ever heard of it?"

"Yes, the name isn't new. What's in this Basin?"

The man grunted. "Tonto once was home for the Apache. It's now got a few sheep an' cattlemen, lots of rustlers. An' say, if you like to hunt bear an' deer, come along with us."

"Thanks. I don't know as I can," returned Tappan, irresolutely. He was not used to such possibilities as this suggested.

Then the woman spoke up. "It's a pretty country. Wild an' different. We live up under the rim rock. There's mineral in the canyons."

Was it that about mineral which decided Tappan or the look in her eyes?

Tappan's world of thought and feeling underwent as great a change as this Tonto Basin differed from the stark desert so long his home. The trail to the log cabin of the Beams climbed many a ridge and slope and foothill, all covered with manzanita, mescal, cedar, and juniper, at last to reach the canyons of the Rim, where lofty pines and spruces lorded it over the under forest of maples and oaks. Though the yellow Rim towered high over the site of the cabin, the altitude was still great, close to seven thousand feet above sea level.

Tappan had fallen in love with this wild wooded and canyoned country. So had Jenet. It was rather funny the way she hung around Tappan, mornings and evenings. She ate luxuriant grass and oak leaves until her sides bulged.

There did not appear to be any flat places in this landscape. Every bench was either up hill or down hill. The Beams had no garden or farm or ranch that Tappan could discover. They raised a few acres of sorghum and corn. Their log cabin was of the most primitive kind, and outfitted poorly. Madge Beam explained that this cabin was their winter abode, and that up on the Rim they had a good house and ranch. Tappan did not inquire closely into anything. If he had interrogated himself, he would have found out that the reason he did not inquire was because he feared something might remove him from the vicinity of Madge Beam. He had thought it strange the Beams avoided wayfarers they had met on the trail, and had gone round a little hamlet Tappan had espied from a hill. Madge Beam, with woman's intuition, had read his mind, and had said: "Jake doesn't get along so well with some of the villagers. An' I've no hankerin' for gun play." That explanation was sufficient for Tappan. He had lived long enough in his wandering years to appreciate that people could have reasons for being solitary.

This trip up into the Rim Rock country bade fair to become Tappan's one and only adventure of the heart. It was not alone the murmuring, clear brook of cold mountain water that enchanted him, nor the stately pines, nor the beautiful silver spruces, nor the wonder of the deep, yellow-walled canyons, so choked with verdure, and haunted by wild creatures. He dared not face his soul, and ask why this dark-eyed woman sought him more and more. Tappan lived in the moment.

He was aware that the few mountaineer neighbors who rode that way rather avoided contact with him. Tappan was not so dense that he did not perceive that the Beams preferred to keep him from outsiders. This perhaps was owing to their desire to sell Tappan the ranch and cattle. Jake offered to let it go at what he called a low figure. Tappan thought it just as well to go out into the forest and hide his bags of gold. He did not trust Jake Beam, and liked less the looks of the men who visited this wilderness ranch. Madge Beam might be related to a rustler, and the associate of rustlers, but that did not necessarily make her a bad woman. Tappan sensed that her attitude was changing, and she seemed to require his respect. At first, all she wanted was his admiration. Tappan's long unused deference for women returned to him, and when he saw that it was having some strange softening effect upon Madge Beam, he redoubled his attentions. They rode and climbed and hunted together. Tappan had pitched his camp not far from the cabin, on a shaded bank of the singing brook. Madge did not leave him much to himself. She was always coming up to his camp, on one pretext or another. Often she would bring two horses, and make Tappan ride with her. Some of these occasions, Tappan saw, occurred while visitors came to the cabin. In three weeks Madge Beam changed from the bold and careless woman who had ridden down into his camp that sunset, to a serious and appealing woman, growing more careful of her person and adornment, and manifestly bearing a burden on her mind.

October came. In the morning white frost glistened on the split-wood shingles of the cabin. The sun soon melted it, and grew warm. The afternoons were still and smoky, melancholy with the enchantment of Indian summer. Tappan hunted wild turkey and deer with Madge, and revived his boyish love of such pursuits. Madge appeared to be a woman of the woods, and had no mean skill with the rifle.

One day they were high on the Rim, with the great timbered basin at their feet. They had come up to hunt deer, but got no farther than the wonderful promontory where before they had lingered.

"Somethin' will happen to me to-day," Madge Beam said, enigmatically.

Tappan never had been much of a talker. But he could listen. The woman unburdened herself this day. She wanted freedom, happiness, a home away from this lonely country, and all the heritage of woman. She confessed it broodingly, passionately. And Tappan recognized truth when he heard it. He was ready to do all in his power for this woman and believed she knew it. But words and acts of sentiment came hard to him.

"Are you goin' to buy Jake's ranch?" she asked.

"I don't know. Is there any hurry?" returned Tappan.

"I reckon not. But I think I'll settle that," she said, decisively.

"How so?"

"Well, Jake hasn't got any ranch," she answered. And added hastily, "No clear title, I mean. He's only homesteaded one hundred an' sixty acres, an' hasn't proved up on it yet. But don't you say I told you."

"Was Jake aimin' to be crooked?"

"I reckon.... An' I was willin' at first. But not now."

Tappan did not speak at once. He saw the woman was in one of her brooding moods. Besides, he wanted to weigh her words. How significant they were! To-day more than ever she had let down. Humility and simplicity seemed to abide with her. And her brooding boded a storm. Tappan's heart swelled in his broad breast. Was life going to dawn rosy and bright for the lonely prospector? He had money to make a home for this woman. What lay in the balance of the hour? Tappan waited, slowly realizing the charged atmosphere.

Madge's somber eyes gazed out over the great void. But, full of thought and passion as they were, they did not see the beauty of that scene. But Tappan saw it. And in some strange sense the color and wildness and sublimity seemed the expression of a new state of his heart. Under him sheered down the ragged and cracked cliffs of the Rim, yellow and gold and gray, full of caves and crevices, ledges for eagles and niches for lions, a thousand feet down to the upward edge of the long green slopes and canyons, and so on down and down into the abyss of forested ravine and ridge, rolling league on league away to the encompassing barrier of purple mountain ranges.

The thickets in the canyons called Tappan's eye back to linger there. How different from the scenes that used to be perpetually in his sight! What riot of color! The tips of the green pines, the crests of the silver spruces, waved about masses of vivid gold of aspen trees, and wonderful cerise and flaming red of maples, and crags of yellow rock, covered with the bronze of frostbitten sumach. Here was autumn and with it the colors of Tappan's favorite season. From below breathed up the low roar of plunging brook; an eagle screeched his wild call; an elk bugled his piercing blast. From the Rim wisps of pine needles blew away on the breeze and fell into the void. A wild country, colorful, beautiful, bountiful. Tappan imagined he could quell his wandering spirit here, with this dark-eyed woman by his side. Never before had Nature so called him. Here was not the cruelty or flinty hardness of the desert. The air was keen and sweet, cold in the shade, warm in the sun. A fragrance of balsam and spruce, spiced with pine, made his breathing a thing of difficulty and delight. How for so many years had he endured vast open spaces without such eye-soothing trees as these? Tappan's back rested against a huge pine that tipped the Rim, and had stood there, stronger than the storms, for many a hundred years. The rock of the promontory was covered with soft brown mats of pine needles. A juniper tree, with its bright green foliage and lilac-colored berries, grew near the pine, and helped to form a secluded little nook, fragrant and somehow haunting. The woman's dark head was close to Tappan, as she sat with her elbows on her knees, gazing down into the basin. Tappan saw the strained tensity of her posture, the heaving of her full bosom. He wondered, while his own emotions, so long darkened, roused to the suspense of that hour.

Suddenly she flung herself into Tappan's arms. The act amazed him. It seemed to have both the passion of a woman and the shame of a girl. Before she hid her face on Tappan's breast he saw how the rich brown had paled, and then flamed.

"Tappan!... Take me away.... Take me away from here—from that life down there," she cried, in smothered voice.

"Madge, you mean take you away—and marry you?" he replied.

"Oh, yes—yes—marry me, if you love me.... I don't see how you can—but you do, don't you?—Say you do."

"I reckon that's what ails me, Madge," he replied, simply.

"*Say* so, then," she burst out.

"All right, I do," said Tappan, with heavy breath. "Madge, words don't come easy for me.... But I think you're wonderful, an' I want you. I haven't dared hope for that, till now. I'm only a wanderer. But it'd be heaven to have you—my wife—an' make a home for you."

"Oh—Oh!" she returned, wildly, and lifted herself to cling round his neck, and to kiss him. "You give me joy.... Oh, Tappan, I love you. I never loved any man before. I know now.... An' I'm not wonderful—or good. But I love you."

The fire of her lips and the clasp of her arms worked havoc in Tappan. No woman had ever loved him, let alone embraced him. To awake suddenly to such rapture as this made him strong and rough in his response. Then all at once she seemed to collapse in his arms and to begin to weep. He feared he had offended or hurt her, and was clumsy in his contrition. Presently she replied:

"Pretty soon—I'll make you—beat me. It's your love—your honesty—that's shamed me.... Tappan, I was party to a trick to—sell you a worthless ranch.... I agreed to—try to make you love me—to fool you—cheat you.... But I've fallen in love with you.—An' my God, I care more for your love—your respect—than for my life. I can't go on with it. I've double-crossed Jake, an' all of them.... Now, am I worth lovin'? Am I worth havin'?"

"More than ever, dear," he said.

"You will take me away?"

"Anywhere—any time, the sooner the better."

She kissed him passionately, and then, disengaging herself from his arms, she knelt and gazed earnestly at him. "I've not told all. I will some day. But I swear now on my soul—I'll be what you think me."

"Madge, you needn't say all that. If you love me—it's enough. More than I ever dreamed of."

"You're a man. Oh, why didn't I meet you when I was eighteen instead of now—twenty-eight, an' all that between.... But enough. A new life begins here for me. We must plan."

"You make the plans an' I'll act on them."

For a moment she was tense and silent, head bowed, hands shut tight. Then she spoke:

"To-night we'll slip away. You make a light pack, that'll go on your saddle. I'll do the same. We'll hide the horses out near where the trail crosses the brook. An' we'll run off—ride out of the country."

Tappan in turn tried to think, but the whirl of his mind made any reason difficult. This dark-eyed, full-bosomed woman loved him, had surrendered herself, asked only his protection. The thing seemed marvelous. Yet she knelt there, those dark eyes on him, infinitely more appealing than ever, haunting with some mystery of sadness and fear he could not divine.

Suddenly Tappan remembered Jenet.

"I must take Jenet," he said.

That startled her. "Jenet—Who's she?"

"My burro."

"Your burro. You can't travel fast with that pack beast. We'll be trailed, an' we'll have to go fast.... You can't take the burro."

Then Tappan was startled. "What! Can't take Jenet?—Why, I—I couldn't get along without her."

"Nonsense. What's a burro? We must ride fast—do you hear?"

"Madge, I'm afraid I—I must take Jenet with me," he said, soberly.

"It's impossible. I can't go if you take her. I tell you I've got to get away. If you want *me* you'll have to leave your precious Jenet behind."

Tappan bowed his head to the inevitable. After all, Jenet was only a beast of burden. She would run wild on the ridges and soon forget him and have no need of him. Something strained in Tappan's breast. He did not see clearly here. This woman was worth more than all else to him.

"I'm stupid, dear," he said. "You see I never before ran off with a beautiful woman.... Of course my burro must be left behind."

Elopement, if such it could be called, was easy for them. Tappan did not understand why Madge wanted to be so secret about it. Was she not free? But then, he reflected, he did not know the circumstances she feared. Besides, he did not care. Possession of the woman was enough.

Tappan made his small pack, the weight of which was considerable owing to his bags of gold. This he tied on his saddle. It bothered him to leave most of his new outfit scattered around his camp. What would Jenet think of that? He looked for her, but for once she did not come in at meal time. Tappan thought this was singular. He could not remember when Jenet had been far from his camp at sunset. Somehow Tappan was glad.

After he had his supper, he left his utensils and supplies as they happened to be, and strode away under the trees to the trysting-place where he was to meet Madge. To his surprise she came before dark, and, unused as he was to the complexity and emotional nature of a woman, he saw that she was strangely agitated. Her face was pale. Almost a fury burned in her black eyes. When she came up to Tappan, and embraced him, almost fiercely, he felt that he was about to learn more of the nature of womankind. She thrilled him to his depths.

"Lead out the horses an' don't make any noise," she whispered.

Tappan complied, and soon he was mounted, riding behind her on the trail. It surprised him that she headed down country, and traveled fast. Moreover, she kept to a trail that continually grew rougher. They came to a road, which she crossed, and kept on through darkness and brush so thick that Tappan could not see the least sign of a trail. And at length anyone could have seen that Madge had lost her bearings. She appeared to know the direction she wanted, but traveling upon it was impossible, owing to the increasingly cut-up and brushy ground. They had to turn back, and seemed to be hours finding the road. Once Tappan fancied he heard the thud of hoofs other than those made by their own horses. Here Madge acted strangely, and where she had been obsessed by desire to hurry she now seemed to have grown weary. She turned her horse south on the road. Tappan was thus enabled to ride beside her. But they talked very little. He was satisfied with the fact of being with her on the way out of the country. Some time in the night they reached an old log shack by the roadside. Here Tappan suggested they halt, and get some sleep before dawn. The morrow would mean a long hard day.

"Yes, to-morrow will be hard," replied Madge, as she faced Tappan in the gloom. He could see her big dark eyes on him. Her tone was not one of a hopeful woman. Tappan pondered over this. But he could not understand, because he had no idea how a woman ought to act under such circumstances. Madge Beam was a creature of moods. Only the day before, on the ride down from the Rim, she had told him with a laugh that she was likely to love him madly one moment and scratch his eyes out the next. How could he know what to make of her? Still, an uneasy feeling began to stir in Tappan.

They dismounted, and unsaddled the horses. Tappan took his pack and put it aside. Something frightened the horses. They bolted down the road.

"Head them off," cried the woman, hoarsely.

Even on the instant her voice sounded strained to Tappan, as if she were choked. But, realizing the absolute necessity of catching the horses, he set off down the road on a run. And he soon succeeded in heading off the animal he had ridden. The other one, however, was contrary and cunning. When Tappan would endeavor to get ahead, it would trot briskly on. Yet it did not go so fast but what Tappan felt sure he would soon catch it. Thus walking and running, he put some distance between him and the cabin before he realized that he could not head off the wary beast. Much perturbed in mind, Tappan hurried back.

Upon reaching the cabin Tappan called to Madge. No answer! He could not see her in the gloom nor the horse he had driven back. Only silence brooded there. Tappan called again. Still no answer! Perhaps Madge had succumbed to weariness and was asleep. A search of the cabin and vicinity failed to yield any sign of her. But it disclosed the fact that Tappan's pack was gone.

Suddenly he sat down, quite overcome. He had been duped. What a fierce pang tore his heart! But it was for loss of the woman—not the gold. He was stunned, and then sick with bitter misery. Only then did Tappan realize the meaning of love and what it had done to him. The night wore on, and he sat there in the dark and cold and stillness until the gray dawn told him of the coming of day.

The light showed his saddle where he had left it. Near by lay one of Madge's gloves. Tappan's keen eye sighted a bit of paper sticking out of the glove. He picked it up. It was a leaf out of a little book he had seen her carry, and upon it was written in lead pencil:

"I am Jake's wife, not his sister. I double-crossed him an'
ran off with you an' would have gone to hell for you. But

- 23 -

Jake an' his gang suspected me. They were close on our trail. I couldn't shake them. So here I chased off the horses an' sent you after them. It was the only way I could save your life."

Tappan tracked the thieves to Globe. There he learned they had gone to Phoenix—three men and one woman. Tappan had money on his person. He bought horse and saddle, and, setting out for Phoenix, he let his passion to kill grow with the miles and hours. At Phoenix he learned Beam had cashed the gold—twelve thousand dollars. So much of a fortune! Tappan's fury grew. The gang separated here. Beam and his wife took stage for Tucson. Tappan had no trouble in trailing their movements.

Gambling dives and inns and freighting posts and stage drivers told the story of the Beams and their ill-gotten gold. They went on to California, down into Tappan's country, to Yuma, and El Cajon, and San Diego. Here Tappan lost track of the woman. He could not find that she had left San Diego, nor any trace of her there. But Jake Beam had killed a Mexican in a brawl and had fled across the line.

Tappan gave up for the time being the chase of Beam, and bent his efforts to find the woman. He had no resentment toward Madge. He only loved her. All that winter he searched San Diego. He made of himself a peddler as a ruse to visit houses. But he never found a trace of her. In the spring he wandered back to Yuma, raking over the old clues, and so on back to Tucson and Phoenix.

This year of dream and love and passion and despair and hate made Tappan old. His great strength and endurance were not yet impaired, but something of his spirit had died out of him.

One day he remembered Jenet. "My burro!" he soliloquized. "I had forgotten her.... Jenet!"

Then it seemed a thousand impulses merged in one drove him to face the long road toward the Rim Rock country. To remember Jenet was to grow doubtful. Of course she would be gone. Stolen or dead or wandered off! But then who could tell what Jenet might do? Tappan was both called and driven. He was a poor wanderer again. His outfit was a pack he carried on his shoulder. But while he could walk he would keep on until he found that last camp where he had deserted Jenet.

October was coloring the canyon slopes when he reached the shadow of the great wall of yellow rock. The cabin where the Beams had lived—or had claimed they lived—was a fallen ruin, crushed by snow. Tappan saw other signs of a severe winter and heavy snowfall. No horse or cattle tracks showed in the trails.

To his amaze his camp was much as he had left it. The stone fireplace, the iron pots, appeared to be in the same places. The boxes that had held his supplies were lying here and there. And his canvas tarpaulin, little the worse for wear of the elements, lay on the ground under the pine where he had slept. If any man had visited this camp in a year he had left no sign of it.

Suddenly Tappan espied a hoof track in the dust. A small track—almost oval in shape—fresh! Tappan thrilled through all his being.

"Jenet's track, so help me God!" he murmured.

He found more of them, made that morning. And, keen now as never before on her trail, he set out to find her. The tracks led up the canyon. Tappan came out into a little grassy clearing, and there stood Jenet, as he had seen her thousands of times. She had both long ears up high. She seemed to stare out of that meek, gray face. And then one of the long ears flopped over and drooped. Such perhaps was the expression of her recognition.

Tappan strode up to her.

"Jenet—old girl—you hung round camp—waitin' for me, didn't you?" he said, huskily, and his big hands fondled her long ears.

Yes, she had waited. She, too, had grown old. She was gray. The winter of that year had been hard. What had she lived on when the snow lay so deep? There were lion scratches on her back, and scars on her legs. She had fought for her life.

"Jenet, a man can never always tell about a burro," said Tappan. "I trained you to hang round camp an' wait till I came back.... 'Tappan's burro,' the desert rats used to say! An' they'd laugh when I bragged how you'd stick to me where most men would quit. But brag as I did, I never knew you, Jenet. An' I left you—an' forgot. Jenet, it takes a human bein'—a man—a woman—to be faithless. An' it takes a dog or a horse or a burro to be great.... Beasts? I wonder now.... Well, old pard, we're goin' down the trail together, an' from this day on Tappan begins to pay his debt."

III

Tappan never again had the old *wanderlust* for the stark and naked desert. Something had transformed him. The green and fragrant forests, and brown-aisled, pine-matted woodlands, the craggy promontories and the great colored canyons, the cold granite water springs of the Tonto seemed vastly preferable to the heat and dust and glare and the emptiness of the waste lands. But there was more. The ghost of his strange and only love kept pace with his wandering steps, a spirit that hovered with him as his shadow. Madge Beam, whatever she had been, had showed to him the power of love to refine and ennoble. Somehow he felt closer to her here in the cliff country where his passion had been born. Somehow she seemed nearer to him here than in all those places he had tracked her.

So from a prospector searching for gold Tappan became a hunter, seeking only the means to keep soul and body together. And all he cared for was his faithful burro Jenet, and the loneliness and silence of the forest land.

He was to learn that the Tonto was a hard country in many ways, and bitterly so in winter. Down in the brakes of the basin it was mild in winter, the snow did not lie long, and ice seldom formed. But up on the Rim, where Tappan always lingered as long as possible, the storm king of the north held full sway. Fifteen feet of snow and zero weather were the rule in dead of winter.

An old native once warned Tappan: "See hyar, friend, I reckon you'd better not get caught up in the Rim Rock country in one of our big storms. Fer if you do you'll never get out."

It was a way of Tappan's to follow his inclinations, regardless of advice. He had weathered the terrible midnight storm of hot wind in Death Valley. What were snow and cold to him? Late autumn on the Rim was the most perfect and beautiful of seasons. He had seen the forest land brown and darkly green one day, and the next burdened with white snow. What a transfiguration! Then when the sun loosened the white mantling on the pines, and they had shed their burdens in drifting dust of white, and rainbowed mists of melting snow, and avalanches sliding off the branches, there would be left only the wonderful white floor of the woodland. The great rugged brown tree trunks appeared mightier and statelier in the contrast; and the green of foliage, the russet of oak leaves, the gold of the aspens, turned the forest into a world enchanting to the desert-seared eyes of this wanderer.

With Tappan the years sped by. His mind grew old faster than his body. Every season saw him lonelier. He had a feeling, a vague illusive foreshadowing that his bones, instead of bleaching on the desert sands, would mingle with the pine mats and the soft fragrant moss of the forest. The idea was pleasant to Tappan.

One afternoon he was camped in Pine Canyon, a timber-sloped gorge far back from the Rim. November was well on. The fall had been singularly open and fair, with not a single storm. A few natives happening across Tappan had remarked casually that such autumns sometimes were not to be trusted.

This late afternoon was one of Indian summer beauty and warmth. The blue haze in the canyon was not all the blue smoke from Tappan's camp-fire. In a narrow park of grass not far from camp Jenet grazed peacefully with elk and deer. Wild turkeys lingered there, loth to seek their winter quarters down in the basin. Gray squirrels and red squirrels barked and frisked, and dropped the pine and spruce cones, with thud and thump, on all the slopes.

Before dark a stranger strode into Tappan's camp, a big man of middle age, whose magnificent physique impressed even Tappan. He was a rugged, bearded giant, wide-eyed and of pleasant face. He had no outfit, no horse, not even a gun.

"Lucky for me I smelled your smoke," he said. "Two days for me without grub."

"Howdy, stranger," was Tappan's greeting. "Are you lost?"

"Yes an' no. I could find my way out down over the Rim, but it's not healthy down there for me. So I'm hittin' north."

"Where's your horse an' pack?"

"I reckon they're with the gang thet took more of a fancy to them than me."

"Ahuh! You're welcome here, stranger," replied Tappan. "I'm Tappan."

"Ha! Heard of you. I'm Jess Blade, of anywhere. An' I'll say, Tappan, I was an honest man till I hit the Tonto."

His laugh was frank, for all its note of grimness. Tappan liked the man, and sensed one who would be a good friend and bad foe.

"Come an' eat. My supplies are peterin' out, but there's plenty of meat."

Blade ate, indeed, as a man starved, and did not seem to care if Tappan's supplies were low. He did not talk. After the meal he craved a pipe and tobacco. Then he smoked in silence, in a slow realizing content. The morrow had no fears for him. The flickering ruddy light from the camp fire shone on his strong face. Tappan saw in him the drifter, the drinker, the brawler, a man with good in him, but over whom evil passion or temper dominated. Presently he smoked the pipe out, and with reluctant hand knocked out the ashes and returned it to Tappan.

"I reckon I've some news thet'd interest you," he said.

"You have?" queried Tappan.

"Yes, if you're the Tappan who tried to run off with Jake Beam's wife."

"Well, I'm that Tappan. But I'd like to say I didn't know she was married."

"Shore, I know thet. So does everybody in the Tonto. You were just meat for thet Beam gang. They had played the trick before. But accordin' to what I hear thet trick was the last fer Madge Beam. She never came back to this

- 27 -

country. An' Jake Beam, when he was drunk, owned up thet she'd left him in California. Some hint at worse. Fer Jake Beam came back a harder man. Even his gang said thet."

"Is he in the Tonto now?" queried Tappan, with a thrill of fire along his veins.

"Yep, thar fer keeps," replied Blade, grimly. "Somebody shot him."

"Ahuh!" exclaimed Tappan with a deep breath of relief. There came a sudden cooling of the heat of his blood.

After that there was a long silence. Tappan dreamed of the woman who had loved him. Blade brooded over the camp fire. The wind moaned fitfully in the lofty pines on the slope. A wolf mourned as if in hunger. The stars appeared to obscure their radiance in haze.

"Reckon thet wind sounds like storm," observed Blade, presently.

"I've heard it for weeks now," replied Tappan.

"Are you a woodsman?"

"No, I'm a desert man."

"Wal, you take my hunch an' hit the trail fer low country."

This was well meant, and probably sound advice, but it alienated Tappan. He had really liked this hearty-voiced stranger. Tappan thought moodily of his slowly ingrowing mind, of the narrowness of his soul. He was past interest in his fellow men. He lived with a dream. The only living creature he loved was a lop-eared, lazy burro, growing old in contentment. Nevertheless that night Tappan shared one of his two blankets.

In the morning the gray dawn broke, and the sun rose without its brightness of gold. There was a haze over the blue sky. Thin, swift-moving clouds scudded up out of the southwest. The wind was chill, the forest shaggy and dark, the birds and squirrels were silent.

"Wal, you'll break camp to-day," asserted Blade.

"Nope. I'll stick it out yet a while," returned Tappan.

"But, man, you might get snowed in, an' up hyar thet's serious."

"Ahuh! Well, it won't bother me. An' there's nothin' holdin' you."

"Tappan, it's four days' walk down out of this woods. If a big snow set in, how'd I make it?"

"Then you'd better go out over the Rim," suggested Tappan.

"No. I'll take my chance the other way. But are you meanin' you'd rather not have me with you? Fer you can't stay hyar."

Tappan was in a quandary.

Some instinct bade him tell the man to go. Not empty-handed, but to go. But this was selfish, and entirely unlike Tappan as he remembered himself of old. Finally he spoke:

"You're welcome to half my outfit—go or stay."

"Thet's mighty square of you, Tappan," responded the other, feelingly. "Have you a burro you'll give me?"

"No, I've only one."

"Ha! Then I'll have to stick with you till you leave."

No more was said. They had breakfast in a strange silence. The wind brooded its secret in the tree tops. Tappan's burro strolled into camp, and caught the stranger's eye.

"Wal, thet's shore a fine burro," he observed. "Never saw the like."

Tappan performed his camp tasks. And then there was nothing to do but sit around the fire. Blade evidently waited for the increasing menace of storm to rouse Tappan to decision. But the graying over of sky and the increase of wind did not affect Tappan. What did he wait for? The truth of his thoughts was that he did not like the way Jenet remained in camp. She was waiting to be packed. She knew they ought to go. Tappan yielded to a perverse devil of stubbornness. The wind brought a cold mist, then a flurry of wet snow. Tappan gathered firewood, a large quantity. Blade saw this and gave voice to earnest fears. But Tappan paid no heed. By nightfall sleet and snow began to fall steadily. The men fashioned a rude shack of spruce boughs, ate their supper, and went to bed early.

It worried Tappan that Jenet stayed right in camp. He lay awake a long time. The wind rose, and moaned through the forest. The sleet failed, and a soft, steady downfall of snow gradually set in. Tappan fell asleep. When he awoke it was to see a forest of white. The trees were mantled with blankets of wet snow, the ground covered two feet on a level. But the clouds appeared to be gone, the sky was blue, the storm over. The sun came up warm and bright.

"It'll all go in a day," said Tappan.

"If this was early October I'd agree with you," replied Blade. "But it's only makin' fer another storm. Can't you hear thet wind?"

Tappan only heard the whispers of his dreams. By now the snow was melting off the pines, and rainbows shone everywhere. Little patches of snow began to drop off the south branches of the pines and spruces, and then larger patches, until by mid-afternoon white streams and avalanches were falling everywhere. All of the snow, except in shaded places on the north sides of trees, went that day, and half of that on the ground. Next day it thinned out more, until Jenet was finding the grass and moss again. That afternoon the telltale thin clouds raced up out of the southwest and the wind moaned its menace.

"Tappan, let's pack an' hit it out of hyar," appealed Blade, anxiously. "I know this country. Mebbe I'm wrong, of course, but it feels like storm. Winter's comin' shore."

"Let her come," replied Tappan, imperturbably.

"Say, do you want to get snowed in?" demanded Blade, out of patience.

"I might like a little spell of it, seein' it'd be new to me," replied Tappan.

"But man, if you ever get snowed in hyar you can't get out."

"That burro of mine could get me out."

"You're crazy. Thet burro couldn't go a hundred feet. What's more, you'd have to kill her an' eat her."

Tappan bent a strange gaze upon his companion, but made no reply. Blade began to pace up and down the small bare patch of ground before the camp fire. Manifestly, he was in a serious predicament. That day he seemed subtly to change, as did Tappan. Both answered to their peculiar instincts, Blade to that of self-preservation, and Tappan, to something like indifference. Tappan held fate in defiance. What more could happen to him?

Blade broke out again, in eloquent persuasion, giving proof of their peril, and from that he passed to amaze and then to strident anger. He cursed Tappan for a nature-loving idiot.

"An' I'll tell you what," he ended. "When mornin' comes I'll take some of your grub an' hit it out of hyar, storm or no storm."

But long before dawn broke that resolution of Blade's had become impracticable. Both men were awakened by a roar of storm through the forest, no longer a moan, but a marching roar, with now a crash and then a shriek of gale! By the light of the smouldering camp fire Tappan saw a whirling pall of snow, great flakes as large as feathers. Morning disclosed the setting in of a fierce mountain storm, with two feet of snow already on the ground, and the forest lost in a blur of white.

"I was wrong," called Tappan to his companion. "What's best to do now?"

"You damned fool!" yelled Blade. "We've got to keep from freezin' an' starvin' till the storm ends an' a crust comes on the snow."

For three days and three nights the blizzard continued, unabated in its fury. It took the men hours to keep a space cleared for their camp site, which Jenet shared with them. On the fourth day the storm ceased, the clouds broke away, the sun came out. And the temperature dropped to zero. Snow on the level just topped Tappan's lofty stature, and in drifts it was ten and fifteen feet deep. Winter had set in without compromise. The forest became a solemn, still, white world. But now Tappan had no time to dream. Dry firewood was hard to find under the snow. It was possible to cut down one of the dead trees on the slope, but impossible to pack sufficient wood to the camp. They had to burn green wood. Then the fashioning of snowshoes took much time. Tappan had no knowledge of such footgear. He could only help Blade. The men were encouraged by the piercing cold forming a crust on the snow. But just as they were about to pack and venture forth, the weather moderated, the crust refused to hold their weight, and another foot of snow fell.

"Why in hell didn't you kill an elk?" demanded Blade, sullenly. He had become darkly sinister. He knew the peril and he loved life. "Now we'll have to kill an' eat your precious Jenet. An' mebbe she won't furnish meat enough to last till this snow weather stops an' a good freeze'll make travelin' possible."

"Blade, you shut up about killin' an' eatin' my burro Jenet," returned Tappan, in a voice that silenced the other.

Thus instinctively these men became enemies. Blade thought only of himself. Tappan had forced upon him a menace to the life of his burro. For himself Tappan had not one thought.

Tappan's supplies ran low. All the bacon and coffee were gone. There was only a small haunch of venison, a bag of beans, a sack of flour, and a small quantity of salt left.

"If a crust freezes on the snow an' we can pack that flour, we'll get out alive," said Blade. "But we can't take the burro."

Another day of bright sunshine softened the snow on the southern exposures, and a night of piercing cold froze a crust that would bear a quick step of man.

"It's our only chance—an' damn slim at thet," declared Blade.

Tappan allowed Blade to choose the time and method, and supplies for the start to get out of the forest. They cooked all the beans and divided them in two sacks. Then they baked about five pounds of biscuits for each of them.

Blade showed his cunning when he chose the small bag of salt for himself and let Tappan take the tobacco. This quantity of food and a blanket for each Blade declared to be all they could pack. They argued over the guns, and in the end Blade compromised on the rifle, agreeing to let Tappan carry that on a possible chance of killing a deer or elk. When this matter had been decided, Blade significantly began putting on his rude snowshoes, that had been constructed from pieces of Tappan's boxes and straps and burlap sacks.

"Reckon they won't last long," muttered Blade.

Meanwhile Tappan fed Jenet some biscuits and then began to strap a tarpaulin on her back.

"What you doin'?" queried Blade, suddenly.

"Gettin' Jenet ready," replied Tappan.

"Ready! For what?"

"Why, to go with us."

"Hell!" shouted Blade, and he threw up his hands in helpless rage.

Tappan felt a depth stirred within him. He lost his late taciturnity and silent aloofness fell away from him. Blade seemed on the moment no longer an enemy. He loomed as an aid to the saving of Jenet. Tappan burst into speech.

"I can't go without her. It'd never enter my head. Jenet's mother was a good faithful burro. I saw Jenet born way down there on the Rio Colorado. She wasn't strong. An' I had to wait for her to be able to walk. An' she grew up. Her mother died, an' Jenet an' me packed it alone. She wasn't no ordinary burro. She learned all I taught her. She was different. But I treated her same as any burro. An' she grew with the years. Desert men said there never was such a burro as Jenet. Called her Tappan's burro, an' tried to borrow an' buy an' steal her.... How many times in ten years Jenet has done me a good turn I can't remember. But she saved my life. She dragged me out of Death Valley.... An' then I forgot my debt. I ran off with a woman an' left Jenet to wait as she had been trained to wait.... Well, I got back in time.... An' now I'll not leave her here. It may be strange to you, Blade, me carin' this way. Jenet's only a burro. But I won't leave her."

"Man, you talk like thet lazy lop-eared burro was a woman," declared Blade, in disgusted astonishment.

"I don't know women, but I reckon Jenet's more faithful than most of them."

"Wal, of all the stark, starin' fools I ever run into you're the worst."

"Fool or not, I know what I'll do," retorted Tappan. The softer mood left him swiftly.

"Haven't you sense enough to see thet we can't travel with your burro?" queried Blade, patiently controlling his temper. "She has little hoofs, sharp as knives. She'll cut through the crust. She'll break through in places. An' we'll have to stop to haul her out—mebbe break through ourselves. Thet would make us longer gettin' out."

"Long or short we'll take her."

Then Blade confronted Tappan as if suddenly unmasking his true meaning. His patient explanation meant nothing. Under no circumstances would he ever have consented to an attempt to take Jenet out of that snow-bound wilderness. His eyes gleamed.

"We've a hard pull to get out alive. An' hard-workin' men in winter must have meat to eat."

Tappan slowly straightened up to look at the speaker.

"What do you mean?"

For answer Blade jerked his hand backward and downward, and when it swung into sight again it held Tappan's worn and shining rifle. Then Blade, with deliberate force, that showed the nature of the man, worked the lever and threw a shell into the magazine. All the while his eyes were fastened on Tappan. His face seemed that of another man, evil, relentless, inevitable in his spirit to preserve his own life at any cost.

"I mean to kill your burro," he said, in voice that suited his look and manner.

"No!" cried Tappan, shocked into an instant of appeal.

"Yes, I am, an' I'll bet, by God, before we get out of hyar you'll be glad to eat some of her meat!"

That roused the slow-gathering might of Tappan's wrath.

"I'd starve to death before I'd—I'd kill that burro, let alone eat her."

"Starve an' be damned!" shouted Blade, yielding to rage.

Jenet stood right behind Tappan, in her posture of contented repose, with one long ear hanging down over her gray meek face.

"You'll have to kill me first," answered Tappan, sharply.

"I'm good fer anythin'—if you push me," returned Blade, stridently.

As he stepped aside, evidently so he could have unobstructed aim at Jenet, Tappan leaped forward and knocked up the rifle as it was discharged. The bullet sped harmlessly over Jenet. Tappan heard it thud into a tree. Blade uttered a curse. And as he lowered the rifle in sudden deadly intent, Tappan grasped the barrel with his left hand. Then, clenching his right, he struck Blade a sodden blow in the face. Only Blade's hold on the rifle prevented him from falling. Blood streamed from his nose and mouth. He bellowed in hoarse fury,

"I'll kill you—fer thet!"

Tappan opened his clenched teeth: "No, Blade—you're not man enough."

Then began a terrific struggle for possession of the rifle. Tappan beat at Blade's face with his sledge-hammer fist. But the strength of the other made it imperative that he use both hands to keep his hold on the rifle. Wrestling and pulling and jerking, the men tore round the snowy camp, scattering the camp fire, knocking down the brush shelter. Blade had surrendered to a wild frenzy. He hissed his maledictions. His was the brute lust to kill an enemy that thwarted him. But Tappan was grim and terrible in his restraint. His battle was to save Jenet. Nevertheless, there mounted in him the hot physical sensations of the savage. The contact of flesh, the smell and sight of Blade's blood, the violent action, the beastly mien of his foe, changed the fight to one for its own sake. To conquer this foe, to rend him and beat him down, blow on blow!

Tappan felt instinctively that he was the stronger. Suddenly he exerted all his muscular force into one tremendous wrench. The rifle broke, leaving the steel barrel in his hands, the wooden stock in Blade's. And it was the quicker-witted Blade who used his weapon first to advantage. One swift blow knocked Tappan down. As he was about to follow it up with another, Tappan kicked his opponent's feet from under him. Blade sprawled in the snow, but was up again as quickly as Tappan. They made at each other, Tappan waiting to strike, and Blade raining blows on Tappan. These were heavy blows aimed at his head, but which he contrived to receive on his arms and the rifle barrel he brandished. For a few moments Tappan stood up under a beating that would have felled a lesser man. His own blood blinded him. Then he swung his heavy weapon. The blow broke Blade's left arm. Like a wild beast, he screamed in pain; and then, without guard, rushed in, too furious for further caution. Tappan met the terrible onslaught as before, and watching his chance, again swung the rifle barrel. This time, so supreme was the force, it battered down Blade's arm and crushed his skull. He died on his feet— ghastly and horrible change!—and swaying backward, he fell into the upbanked wall of snow, and went out of sight, except for his boots, one of which still held the crude snowshoe.

Tappan stared, slowly realizing.

"Ahuh, stranger Blade!" he ejaculated, gazing at the hole in the snow bank where his foe had disappeared. "You were goin' to—kill an' eat—Tappan's burro!"

Then he sighted the bloody rifle barrel, and cast it from him. He became conscious of injuries which needed attention. But he could do little more than wash off the blood and bind up his head. Both arms and hands were badly bruised, and beginning to swell. But fortunately no bones had been broken.

Tappan finished strapping the tarpaulin upon the burro; and, taking up both his and Blade's supply of food, he called out, "Come on, Jenet."

Which way to go! Indeed, there was no more choice for him than there had been for Blade. Towards the Rim the snowdrift would be deeper and impassable. Tappan realized that the only possible chance for him was down hill. So he led Jenet out of camp without looking back once. What was it that had happened? He did not seem to be the same Tappan that had dreamily tramped into this woodland.

A deep furrow in the snow had been made by the men packing firewood into camp. At the end of this furrow the wall of snow stood higher than Tappan's head. To get out on top without breaking the crust presented a problem. He lifted Jenet up, and was relieved to see that the snow held her. But he found a different task in his own case. Returning to camp, he gathered up several of the long branches of spruce that had been part of the shelter, and carrying them out he laid them against the slant of snow he had to surmount, and by their aid he got on top. The crust held him.

Elated and with revived hope, he took up Jenet's halter and started off. Walking with his rude snowshoes was awkward. He had to go slowly, and slide them along the crust. But he progressed. Jenet's little steps kept her even with him. Now and then one of her sharp hoofs cut through, but not to hinder her particularly. Right at the start Tappan observed a singular something about Jenet. Never until now had she been dependent upon him. She knew it. Her intelligence apparently told her that if she got out of this snow-bound wilderness it would be owing to the strength and reason of her master.

Tappan kept to the north side of the canyon, where the snow crust was strongest. What he must do was to work up to the top of the canyon slope, and then keeping to the ridge travel north along it, and so down out of the forest.

Travel was slow. He soon found he had to pick his way. Jenet appeared to be absolutely unable to sense either danger or safety. Her experience had been of the rock confines and the drifting sands of the desert. She walked where Tappan led her. And it seemed to Tappan that her trust in him, her reliance upon him, were pathetic.

"Well, old girl," said Tappan to her, "it's a horse of another color now—hey?"

At length he came to a wide part of the canyon, where a bench of land led to a long gradual slope, thickly studded with small pines. This appeared to be fortunate, and turned out to be so, for when Jenet broke through the crust Tappan had trees and branches to hold to while he hauled her out. The labor of climbing that slope was such that Tappan began to appreciate Blade's absolute refusal to attempt getting Jenet out. Dusk was shadowing the white aisles of the forest when Tappan ascended to a level. He had not traveled far from camp, and the fact struck a chill upon his heart.

To go on in the dark was foolhardy. So Tappan selected a thick spruce, under which there was a considerable depression in the snow, and here made preparation to spend the night. Unstrapping the tarpaulin, he spread it on the snow. All the lower branches of this giant of the forest were dead and dry. Tappan broke off many and soon had a fire. Jenet nibbled at the moss on the trunk of the spruce tree. Tappan's meal consisted of beans, biscuits, and a ball of snow, that he held over the fire to soften. He saw to it that Jenet fared as well as he. Night soon fell, strange and weirdly white in the forest, and piercingly cold. Tappan needed the fire. Gradually it melted the snow and made a hole, down to the ground. Tappan rolled up in the tarpaulin and soon fell asleep.

In three days Tappan traveled about fifteen miles, gradually descending, until the snow crust began to fail to hold Jenet. Then whatever had been his difficulties before, they were now magnified a hundredfold. As soon as the sun was up, somewhat softening the snow, Jenet began to break through. And often when Tappan began hauling her out he broke through himself. This exertion was killing even to a man of Tappan's physical prowess. The endurance to resist heat and flying dust and dragging sand seemed another kind from that needed to toil on in this snow. The endless snow-bound forest began to be hideous to Tappan. Cold, lonely, dreary, white, mournful—the kind of ghastly and ghostly winter land that had been the terror of Tappan's boyish dreams! He loved the sun—the open. This forest had deceived him. It was a wall of ice. As he toiled on, the state of his mind gradually and subtly changed in all except the fixed and absolute will to save Jenet. In some places he carried her.

The fourth night found him dangerously near the end of his stock of food. He had been generous with Jenet. But now, considering that he had to do more work than she, he diminished her share. On the fifth day Jenet broke through the snow crust so often that Tappan realized how utterly impossible it was for her to get out of the woods by her own efforts. Therefore Tappan hit upon the plan of making her lie on the tarpaulin, so that he could drag her. The tarpaulin doubled once did not make a bad sled. All the rest of that day Tappan hauled her. And so all the rest of the next day he toiled on, hands behind him, clutching the canvas, head and shoulders bent, plodding and methodical, like a man who could not be defeated. That night he was too weary to build a fire, and too worried to eat the last of his food.

Next day Tappan was not unalive to the changing character of the forest. He had worked down out of the zone of the spruce trees; the pines had thinned out and decreased in size; oak trees began to show prominently. All these signs meant that he was getting down out of the mountain heights. But the fact, hopeful as it was, had drawbacks. The snow was still four feet deep on a level and the crust held Tappan only about half the time. Moreover, the lay of the land operated against Tappan's progress. The long, slowly descending ridge had failed. There were no more canyons, but ravines and swales were numerous. Tappan dragged on, stern, indomitable, bent to his toil.

When the crust let him down, he hung his snowshoes over Jenet's back, and wallowed through, making a lane for her to follow. Two days of such heart-breaking toil, without food or fire, broke Tappan's magnificent endurance. But not his spirit! He hauled Jenet over the snow, and through the snow, down the hills and up the slopes, through the thickets, knowing that over the next ridge, perhaps, was deliverance. Deer and elk tracks began to be numerous. Cedar and juniper trees now predominated. An occasional pine showed here and there. He was getting out of the forest land. Only such mighty and justifiable hope as that could have kept him on his feet.

He fell often, and it grew harder to rise and go on. The hour came when the crust failed altogether to hold Tappan, and he had to abandon hauling Jenet. It was necessary to make a road for her. How weary, cold, horrible, the white reaches! Yard by yard Tappan made his way. He no longer sweat. He had no feeling in his feet or legs. Hunger ceased to gnaw at his vitals. His thirst he quenched with snow—soft snow now, that did not have to be crunched like ice. The pangs in his breast were terrible—cramps, constrictions, the piercing pains in his lungs, the dull ache of his overtaxed heart.

Tappan came to an opening in the cedar forest from which he could see afar. A long slope fronted him. It led down and down to open country. His desert eyes, keen as those of an eagle, made out flat country, sparsely covered with snow, and black dots that were cattle. The last slope! The last pull! Three feet of snow, except in drifts; down and down he plunged, making way for Jenet!

All that day he toiled and fell and rolled down this league-long slope, wearing towards sunset to the end of his task, and likewise to the end of his will.

Now he seemed up and now down. There was no sense of cold or weariness. Only direction! Tappan still saw! The last of his horror at the monotony of white faded from his mind. Jenet was there, beginning to be able to travel for herself. The solemn close of endless day found Tappan arriving at the edge of the timbered country, where wind-bared patches of ground showed long, bleached grass. Jenet took to grazing.

As for Tappan, he fell with the tarpaulin, under a thick cedar, and with strengthless hands plucked and plucked at the canvas to spread it, so that he could cover himself. He looked again for Jenet. She was there, somehow a fading image, strangely blurred. But she was grazing. Tappan lay down, and stretched out, and slowly drew the tarpaulin over him.

A piercing cold night wind swept down from the snowy heights. It wailed in the edge of the cedars and moaned out towards the open country. Yet the night seemed silent. The stars shone white in a deep blue sky—passionless, cold, watchful eyes, looking down without pity or hope or censure. They were the eyes of Nature. Winter had locked the heights in its snowy grip. All night that winter wind blew down, colder and colder. Then dawn broke, steely, gray, with a flare in the east.

Jenet came back where she had left her master. Camp! As she had returned thousands of dawns in the long years of her service. She had grazed all night. Her sides that had been flat were now full. Jenet had weathered another vicissitude of her life. She stood for a while, in a doze, with one long ear down over her meek face. Jenet was waiting for Tappan.

But he did not stir from under the long roll of canvas. Jenet waited. The winter sun rose, in cold yellow flare. The snow glistened as with a crusting of diamonds. Somewhere in the distance sounded a long-drawn, discordant bray. Jenet's ears shot up. She listened. She recognized the call of one of her kind. Instinct always prompted Jenet. Sometimes she did bray. Lifting her gray head she sent forth a clarion: "*Hee-haw hee-haw-haw—hee-haw how-e-e-e!*"

That stentorian call started the echoes. They pealed down the slope and rolled out over the open country, clear as a bugle blast, yet hideous in their discordance. But this morning Tappan did not awaken.

THE GREAT SLAVE

A VOICE on the wind whispered to Siena the prophecy of his birth. "A chief is born to save the vanishing tribe of Crows! A hunter to his starving people!" While he listened, at his feet swept swift waters, the rushing, green-white, thundering Athabasca, spirit-forsaken river; and it rumbled his name and murmured his fate. "Siena! Siena! His bride will rise from a wind kiss on the flowers in the moonlight! A new land calls to the last of the Crows! Northward where the wild goose ends its flight Siena will father a great people!"

So Siena, a hunter of the leafy trails, dreamed his dreams; and at sixteen he was the hope of the remnant of a once powerful tribe, a stripling chief, beautiful as a bronzed autumn god, silent, proud, forever listening to voices on the wind.

To Siena the lore of the woodland came as flight comes to the strong-winged wild fowl. The secrets of the forests were his, and of the rocks and rivers.

He knew how to find the nests of the plover, to call the loon, to net the heron, and spear the fish. He understood the language of the whispering pines. Where the deer came down to drink and the caribou browsed on moss and the white rabbit nibbled in the grass and the bear dug in the logs for grubs—all these he learned; and also when the black flies drove the moose into the water and when the honk of the geese meant the approach of the north wind.

He lived in the woods, with his bow, his net, and his spear. The trees were his brothers. The loon laughed for his happiness, the wolf mourned for his sadness. The bold crag above the river, Old Stoneface, heard his step when he climbed there in the twilight. He communed with the stern god of his ancestors and watched the flashing Northern Lights and listened.

From all four corners came his spirit guides with steps of destiny on his trail. On all the four winds breathed voices whispering of his future; loudest of all called the Athabasca, god-forsaken river, murmuring of the bride born of a wind kiss on the flowers in the moonlight.

ON ALL THE FOUR WINDS BREATHED VOICES
WHISPERING OF HIS FUTURE

It was autumn, with the flame of leaf fading, the haze rolling out of the hollows, the lull yielding to moan of coming wind. All the signs of a severe winter were in the hulls of the nuts, in the fur of the foxes, in the flight of water-fowl. Siena was spearing fish for winter store. None so keen of sight as Siena, so swift of arm; and as he was the hope, so he alone was the provider for the starving tribe. Siena stood to his knees in a brook where it flowed over its gravelly bed into the Athabasca. Poised high was his wooden spear. It glinted downward swift as a shaft of sunlight through the leaves. Then Siena lifted a quivering whitefish and tossed it upon the bank where his mother Ema, with other women of the tribe, sun-dried the fish upon a rock.

Again and again, many times, flashed the spear. The young chief seldom missed his aim. Early frosts on the uplands had driven the fish down to deeper water, and as they came darting over the bright pebbles Siena called them by name.

The oldest squaw could not remember such a run of fish. Ema sang the praises of her son; the other women ceased the hunger chant of the tribe.

Suddenly a hoarse shout pealed out over the waters.

Ema fell in a fright; her companions ran away; Siena leaped upon the bank, clutching his spear. A boat in which were men with white faces drifted down toward him.

"Hal-loa!" again sounded the hoarse cry.

Ema cowered in the grass. Siena saw a waving of white hands; his knees knocked together and he felt himself about to flee. But Siena of the Crows, the savior of a vanishing tribe, must not fly from visible foes.

"Palefaces," he whispered, trembling, yet stood his ground ready to fight for his mother. He remembered stories of an old Indian who had journeyed far to the south and had crossed the trails of the dreaded white men. There stirred in him vague memories of strange Indian runners telling camp-fire tales of white hunters with weapons of lightning and thunder.

"Naza! Naza!" Siena cast one fleeting glance to the north and a prayer to his god of gods. He believed his spirit would soon be wandering in the shades of the other Indian world.

As the boat beached on the sand Siena saw men lying with pale faces upward to the sky, and voices in an unknown tongue greeted him. The tone was friendly, and he lowered his threatening spear. Then a man came up the bank, his hungry eyes on the pile of fish, and he began to speak haltingly in mingled Cree and Chippewayan language:

"Boy—we're white friends—starving—let us buy fish—trade for fish— we're starving and we have many moons to travel."

"Siena's tribe is poor," replied the lad; "sometimes they starve too. But Siena will divide his fish and wants no trade."

His mother, seeing the white men intended no evil, came out of her fright and complained bitterly to Siena of his liberality. She spoke of the menacing winter, of the frozen streams, the snow-bound forest, the long night of hunger. Siena silenced her and waved the frightened braves and squaws back to their wigwams.

"Siena is young," he said simply; "but he is chief here. If we starve—we starve."

Whereupon he portioned out a half of the fish. The white men built a fire and sat around it feasting like famished wolves around a fallen stag. When they had appeased their hunger they packed the remaining fish in the boat, whistling and singing the while. Then the leader made offer to pay, which Siena refused, though the covetous light in his mother's eyes hurt him sorely.

"Chief," said the leader, "the white man understands; now he offers presents as one chief to another."

Thereupon he proffered bright beads and tinseled trinkets, yards of calico and strips of cloth. Siena accepted with a dignity in marked contrast to the way in which the greedy Ema pounced upon the glittering heap. Next the paleface presented a knife which, drawn from its scabbard, showed a blade that mirrored its brightness in Siena's eyes.

"Chief, your woman complains of a starving tribe," went on the white man. "Are there not many moose and reindeer?"

"Yes. But seldom can Siena creep within range of his arrow."

"A-ha! Siena will starve no more," replied the man, and from the boat he took a long iron tube with a wooden stock.

"What is that?" asked Siena.

"The wonderful shooting stick. Here, boy, watch! See the bark on the camp fire. Watch!"

He raised the stick to his shoulder. Then followed a streak of flame, a puff of smoke, a booming report; and the bark of the camp fire flew into bits.

The children dodged into the wigwams with loud cries, the women ran screaming, Ema dropped in the grass wailing that the end of the world had come, while Siena, unable to move hand or foot, breathed another prayer to Naza of the northland.

The white man laughed and, patting Siena's arm, he said: "No fear." Then he drew Siena away from the bank, and began to explain the meaning and use of the wonderful shooting stick. He reloaded it and fired again and yet again, until Siena understood and was all aflame at the possibilities of such a weapon.

Patiently the white man taught the Indian how to load it, sight, and shoot, and how to clean it with ramrod and buckskin. Next he placed at Siena's feet a keg of powder, a bag of lead bullets, and boxes full of caps. Then he bade Siena farewell, entered the boat with his men and drifted round a bend of the swift Athabasca.

Siena stood alone upon the bank, the wonderful shooting stick in his hands, and the wail of his frightened mother in his ears. He comforted her, telling her the white men were gone, that he was safe, and that the prophecy of his birth had at last begun its fulfillment. He carried the precious ammunition to a safe hiding place in a hollow log near his wigwam and then he plunged into the forest.

Siena bent his course toward the runways of the moose. He walked in a kind of dream, for he both feared and believed. Soon the glimmer of water, splashes and widening ripples, caused him to crawl stealthily through the ferns and grasses to the border of a pond. The familiar hum of flies told him of the location of his quarry. The moose had taken to the water, driven by the swarms of black flies, and were standing neck deep, lifting their muzzles to feed on the drooping poplar branches. Their wide-spreading antlers, tipped back into the water, made the ripples.

Trembling as never before, Siena sank behind a log. He was within fifty paces of the moose. How often in that very spot had he strung a feathered arrow and shot it vainly! But now he had the white man's weapon, charged with lightning and thunder. Just then the poplars parted above the shore, disclosing a bull in the act of stepping down. He tossed his antlered head at the cloud of humming flies, then stopped, lifting his nose to scent the wind.

"Naza!" whispered Siena in his swelling throat.

He rested the shooting stick on the log and tried to see over the brown barrel. But his eyes were dim. Again he whispered a prayer to Naza. His sight cleared, his shaking arms stilled, and with his soul waiting, hoping, doubting, he aimed and pulled the trigger.

Boom!

High the moose flung his ponderous head, to crash down upon his knees, to roll in the water and churn a bloody foam, and then lie still.

"Siena! Siena!"

Shrill the young chief's exultant yell pealed over the listening waters, piercing the still forest, to ring back in echo from Old Stoneface. It was Siena's triumphant call to his forefathers, watching him from the silence.

The herd of moose plowed out of the pond and crashed into the woods, where, long after they had disappeared, their antlers could be heard cracking the saplings.

When Siena stood over the dead moose his doubts fled; he was indeed god-chosen. No longer chief of a starving tribe! Reverently and with immutable promise he raised the shooting stick to the north, toward Naza who had remembered him; and on the south, where dwelt the enemies of his tribe, his dark glance brooded wild and proud and savage.

Eight times the shooting stick boomed out in the stillness and eight moose lay dead in the wet grasses. In the twilight Siena wended his way home and placed eight moose tongues before the whimpering squaws.

"Siena is no longer a boy," he said. "Siena is a hunter. Let his women go bring in the meat."

Then to the rejoicing and feasting and dancing of his tribe he turned a deaf ear, and in the night passed alone under the shadow of Old Stoneface, where he walked with the spirits of his ancestors and believed the voices on the wind.

Before the ice locked the ponds Siena killed a hundred moose and reindeer. Meat and fat and oil and robes changed the world for the Crow tribe.

Fires burned brightly all the long winter; the braves awoke from their stupor and chanted no more; the women sang of the Siena who had come, and prayed for summer wind and moonlight to bring his bride.

Spring went by, summer grew into blazing autumn, and Siena's fame and the wonder of the shooting stick spread through the length and breadth of the land.

Another year passed, then another, and Siena was the great chief of the rejuvenated Crows. He had grown into a warrior's stature, his face had the beauty of the god-chosen, his eye the falcon flash of the Sienas of old. Long communion in the shadow of Old Stoneface had added wisdom to his other gifts; and now to his worshiping tribe all that was needed to complete the prophecy of his birth was the coming of the alien bride.

It was another autumn, with the wind whipping the tamaracks and moaning in the pines, and Siena stole along a brown, fern-lined trail. The dry smell of fallen leaves filled his nostrils; he tasted snow in the keen breezes. The flowers were dead, and still no dark-eyed bride sat in his wigwam. Siena sorrowed and strengthened his heart to wait. He saw her flitting in the shadows around him, a wraith with dusky eyes veiled by dusky wind-blown hair, and ever she hovered near him, whispering from every dark pine, from every waving tuft of grass.

To her whispers he replied: "Siena waits."

He wondered of what alien tribe she would come. He hoped not of the unfriendly Chippewayans or the far-distant Blackfeet; surely not of the hostile Crees, life enemies of his tribe, destroyers of its once puissant strength, jealous now of its resurging power.

Other shadows flitted through the forest, spirits that rose silently from the graves over which he trod, and warned him of double steps on his trail, of unseen foes watching him from the dark coverts. His braves had repeated gossip, filterings from stray Indian wanderers, hinting of plots against the risen Siena. To all these he gave no heed, for was not he Siena, god-chosen, and had he not the wonderful shooting stick?

It was the season that he loved, when dim forest and hazy fernland spoke most impellingly. The tamaracks talked to him, the poplars bowed as he passed, and the pines sang for him alone. The dying vines twined about his feet and clung to him, and the brown ferns, curling sadly, waved him a welcome that was a farewell. A bird twittered a plaintive note and a loon whistled a lonely call. Across the wide gray hollows and meadows of white moss moaned the north wind, bending all before it, blowing full into Siena's face with its bitter promise. The lichen-covered rocks and the rugged-barked trees and the creatures that moved among them—the whole world of earth and air heard Siena's step on the rustling leaves and a thousand voices hummed in the autumn stillness.

So he passed through the shadowy forest and over the gray muskeg flats to his hunting place. With his birch-bark horn he blew the call of the moose. He alone of hunting Indians had the perfect moose call. There, hidden within a thicket, he waited, calling and listening till an angry reply bellowed from the depths of a hollow, and a bull moose, snorting fight, came cracking the saplings in his rush. When he sprang fierce and bristling into the glade, Siena killed him. Then, laying his shooting stick over a log, he drew his knife and approached the beast.

A snapping of twigs alarmed Siena and he whirled upon the defensive, but too late to save himself. A band of Indians pounced upon him and bore him to the ground. One wrestling heave Siena made, then he was overpowered and bound. Looking upward, he knew his captors, though he had never seen them before; they were the lifelong foes of his people, the fighting Crees.

A sturdy chief, bronze of face and sinister of eye, looked grimly down upon his captive. "Baroma makes Siena a slave."

———

Siena and his tribe were dragged far southward to the land of the Crees. The young chief was bound upon a block in the center of the village where hundreds of Crees spat upon him, beat him, and outraged him in every way their cunning could devise. Siena's gaze was on the north and his face showed no sign that he felt the torments.

At last Baroma's old advisers stopped the spectacle, saying: "This is a man!"

Siena and his people became slaves of the Crees. In Baroma's lodge, hung upon caribou antlers, was the wonderful shooting stick with Siena's powder horn and bullet pouch, objects of intense curiosity and fear.

None knew the mystery of this lightning-flashing, thunder-dealing thing; none dared touch it.

The heart of Siena was broken; not for his shattered dreams or the end of his freedom, but for his people. His fame had been their undoing. Slaves to the murderers of his forefathers! His spirit darkened, his soul sickened; no more did sweet voices sing to him on the wind, and his mind dwelt apart from his body among shadows and dim shapes.

Because of his strength he was worked like a dog at hauling packs and carrying wood; because of his fame he was set to cleaning fish and washing vessels with the squaws. Seldom did he get to speak a word to his mother or any of his people. Always he was driven.

One day, when he lagged almost fainting, a maiden brought him water to drink. Siena looked up, and all about him suddenly brightened, as when sunlight bursts from cloud.

"Who is kind to Siena?" he asked, drinking.

"Baroma's daughter," replied the maiden.

"What is her name?"

Quickly the maiden bent her head, veiling dusky eyes with dusky hair. "Emihiyah."

"Siena has wandered on lonely trails and listened to voices not meant for other ears. He has heard the music of Emihiyah on the winds. Let the daughter of Siena's great foe not fear to tell of her name."

"Emihiyah means a wind kiss on the flowers in the moonlight," she whispered shyly and fled.

Love came to the last of the Sienas and it was like a glory. Death shuddered no more in Siena's soul. He saw into the future, and out of his gloom he rose again, god-chosen in his own sight, with such added beauty to his stern face and power to his piercing eye and strength to his lofty frame that the Crees quailed before him and marveled. Once more sweet voices came to him, and ever on the soft winds were songs of the dewy moorlands to the northward, songs of the pines and the laugh of the loon and of the rushing, green-white, thundering Athabasca, god-forsaken river.

Siena's people saw him strong and patient, and they toiled on, unbroken, faithful. While he lived, the pride of Baroma was vaunting. "Siena waits" were the simple words he said to his mother, and she repeated them as wisdom.

But the flame of his eye was like the leaping Northern Lights, and it kept alive the fire deep down in their breasts.

In the winter when the Crees lolled in their wigwams, when less labor fell to Siena, he set traps in the snow trails for silver fox and marten. No Cree had ever been such a trapper as Siena. In the long months he captured many furs, with which he wrought a robe the like of which had not before been the delight of a maiden's eye. He kept it by him for seven nights, and always during this time his ear was turned to the wind. The seventh night was the night of the midwinter feast, and when the torches burned bright in front of Baroma's lodge Siena took the robe and, passing slowly and stately till he stood before Emihiyah, he laid it at her feet.

Emihiyah's dusky face paled, her eyes that shone like stars drooped behind her flying hair, and all her slender body trembled.

"Slave!" cried Baroma, leaping erect. "Come closer that Baroma may see what kind of a dog approaches Emihiyah."

Siena met Baroma's gaze, but spoke no word. His gift spoke for him. The hated slave had dared to ask in marriage the hand of the proud Baroma's daughter. Siena towered in the firelight with something in his presence that for a moment awed beholders. Then the passionate and untried braves broke the silence with a clamor of the wolf pack.

Tillimanqua, wild son of Baroma, strung an arrow to his bow and shot it into Siena's hip, where it stuck, with feathered shaft quivering.

The spring of the panther was not swifter than Siena; he tossed Tillimanqua into the air and, flinging him down, trod on his neck and wrenched the bow away. Siena pealed out the long-drawn war whoop of his tribe that had not been heard for a hundred years, and the terrible cry stiffened the Crees in their tracks.

Then he plucked the arrow from his hip and, fitting it to the string, pointed the gory flint head at Tillimanqua's eyes and began to bend the bow. He bent the tough wood till the ends almost met, a feat of exceeding great strength, and thus he stood with brawny arms knotted and stretched.

A scream rent the suspense. Emihiyah fell upon her knees. "Spare Emihiyah's brother!"

Siena cast one glance at the kneeling maiden, then, twanging the bow string, he shot the arrow toward the sky.

"Baroma's slave is Siena," he said, with scorn like the lash of a whip. "Let the Cree learn wisdom."

Then Siena strode away, with a stream of dark blood down his thigh, and went to his brush tepee, where he closed his wound.

In the still watches of the night, when the stars blinked through the leaves and the dew fell, when Siena burned and throbbed in pain, a shadow passed between his weary eyes and the pale light. And a voice that was not one of the spirit voices on the wind called softly over him, "Siena! Emihiyah comes."

The maiden bound the hot thigh with a soothing balm and bathed his fevered brow.

Then her hands found his in tender touch, her dark face bent low to his, her hair lay upon his cheek. "Emihiyah keeps the robe," she said.

"Siena loves Emihiyah," he replied.

"Emihiyah loves Siena," she whispered.

She kissed him and stole away.

On the morrow Siena's wound was as if it had never been; no eye saw his pain. Siena returned to his work and his trapping. The winter melted into spring, spring flowered into summer, summer withered into autumn.

Once in the melancholy days Siena visited Baroma in his wigwam. "Baroma's hunters are slow. Siena sees a famine in the land."

"Let Baroma's slave keep his place among the squaws," was the reply.

That autumn the north wind came a moon before the Crees expected it; the reindeer took their annual march farther south; the moose herded warily in open groves; the whitefish did not run, and the seven-year pest depleted the rabbits.

When the first snow fell Baroma called a council and then sent his hunting braves far and wide.

One by one they straggled back to camp, footsore and hungry, and each with the same story. It was too late.

A few moose were in the forest, but they were wild and kept far out of range of the hunter's arrows, and there was no other game.

A blizzard clapped down upon the camp, and sleet and snow whitened the forest and filled the trails. Then winter froze everything in icy clutch. The old year drew to a close.

The Crees were on the brink of famine. All day and all night they kept up their chanting and incantations and beating of tom-toms to conjure the return of the reindeer. But no reindeer appeared.

It was then that the stubborn Baroma yielded to his advisers and consented to let Siena save them from starvation by means of his wonderful shooting stick. Accordingly Baroma sent word to Siena to appear at his wigwam.

Siena did not go, and said to the medicine men: "Tell Baroma soon it will be for Siena to demand."

Then the Cree chieftain stormed and stamped in his wigwam and swore away the life of his slave. Yet again the wise medicine men prevailed. Siena and the wonderful shooting stick would be the salvation of the Crees. Baroma, muttering deep in his throat like distant thunder, gave sentence to starve Siena until he volunteered to go forth to hunt, or let him be the first to die.

The last scraps of meat, except a little hoarded in Baroma's lodge, were devoured, and then began the boiling of bones and skins to make a soup to sustain life. The cold days passed and a silent gloom pervaded the camp. Sometimes a cry of a bereaved mother, mourning for a starved child, wailed through the darkness. Siena's people, long used to starvation, did not suffer or grow weak so soon as the Crees. They were of hardier frame, and they were upheld by faith in their chief. When he would sicken it would be time for them to despair. But Siena walked erect as in the days of his freedom, nor did he stagger under the loads of firewood, and there was a light on his face. The Crees, knowing of Baroma's order that Siena should be the first to perish of starvation, gazed at the slave first in awe, then in fear. The last of the Sienas was succored by the spirits.

But god-chosen though Siena deemed himself, he knew it was not by the spirits that he was fed in this time of famine. At night in the dead stillness, when even no mourning of wolf came over the frozen wilderness, Siena lay in his brush tepee close and warm under his blanket. The wind was faint and low, yet still it brought the old familiar voices. And it bore another sound— the soft fall of a moccasin on the snow. A shadow passed between Siena's eyes and the pale light.

"Emihiyah comes," whispered the shadow and knelt over him.

She tendered a slice of meat which she had stolen from Baroma's scant hoard as he muttered and growled in uneasy slumber. Every night since her father's order to starve Siena, Emihiyah had made this perilous errand.

And now her hand sought his and her dusky hair swept his brow. "Emihiyah is faithful," she breathed low.

"Siena only waits," he replied.

She kissed him and stole away.

Cruel days fell upon the Crees before Baroma's pride was broken. Many children died and some of the mothers were beyond help. Siena's people kept their strength, and he himself showed no effect of hunger. Long ago the Cree women had deemed him superhuman, that the Great Spirit fed him from the happy hunting grounds.

At last Baroma went to Siena. "Siena may save his people and the Crees."

Siena regarded him long, then replied: "Siena waits."

"Let Baroma know. What does Siena wait for? While he waits we die."

Siena smiled his slow, inscrutable smile and turned away.

Baroma sent for his daughter and ordered her to plead for her life.

Emihiyah came, fragile as a swaying reed, more beautiful than a rose choked in a tangled thicket, and she stood before Siena with doe eyes veiled. "Emihiyah begs Siena to save her and the tribe of Crees."

"Siena waits," replied the slave.

Baroma roared in his fury and bade his braves lash the slave. But the blows fell from feeble arms and Siena laughed at his captors.

Then, like a wild lion unleashed from long thrall, he turned upon them: "Starve! Cree dogs! Starve! When the Crees all fall like leaves in autumn, then Siena and his people will go back to the north."

Baroma's arrogance left him then, and on another day, when Emihiyah lay weak and pallid in his wigwam and the pangs of hunger gnawed at his own vitals, he again sought Siena. "Let Siena tell for what he waits."

Siena rose to his lofty height and the leaping flame of the Northern Light gathered in his eyes. "Freedom!" One word he spoke and it rolled away on the wind.

"Baroma yields," replied the Cree, and hung his head.

"Send the squaws who can walk and the braves who can crawl out upon Siena's trail."

Then Siena went to Baroma's lodge and took up the wonderful shooting stick and, loading it, he set out upon snowshoes into the white forest. He knew where to find the moose yards in the sheltered corners. He heard the bulls pounding the hard-packed snow and cracking their antlers on the trees. The wary beasts would not have allowed him to steal close, as a warrior armed with a bow must have done, but Siena fired into the herd at long range. And when they dashed off, sending the snow up like a spray, a huge black bull lay dead. Siena followed them as they floundered through the drifts, and whenever he came within range he shot again. When five moose were killed he turned upon his trail to find almost the whole Cree tribe had followed him and were tearing the meat and crying out in a kind of crazy joy. That night the fires burned before the wigwams, the earthen pots steamed, and there was great rejoicing. Siena hunted the next day, and the next, and for ten days he went into the white forest with his wonderful shooting stick, and eighty moose fell to his unerring aim.

The famine was broken and the Crees were saved.

When the mad dances ended and the feasts were over, Siena appeared before Baroma's lodge. "Siena will lead his people northward."

Baroma, starving, was a different chief from Baroma well fed and in no pain. All his cunning had returned. "Siena goes free. Baroma gave his word. But Siena's people remain slaves."

"Siena demanded freedom for himself and people," said the younger chief.

"Baroma heard no word of Siena's tribe. He would not have granted freedom for them. Siena's freedom was enough."

"The Cree twists the truth. He knows Siena would not go without his people. Siena might have remembered Baroma's cunning. The Crees were ever liars."

Baroma stalked before his fire with haughty presence. About him in the circle of light sat his medicine men, his braves and squaws. "The Cree is kind. He gave his word. Siena is free. Let him take his wonderful shooting stick and go back to the north."

Siena laid the shooting stick at Baroma's feet and likewise the powder horn and bullet pouch. Then he folded his arms, and his falcon eyes looked far beyond Baroma to the land of the changing lights and the old home on the green-white, rushing Athabasca, god-forsaken river. "Siena stays."

Baroma started in amaze and anger. "Siena makes Baroma's word idle. Begone!"

"Siena stays!"

The look of Siena, the pealing reply, for a moment held the chief mute. Slowly Baroma stretched wide his arms and lifted them, while from his face flashed a sullen wonder. "Great Slave!" he thundered.

So was respect forced from the soul of the Cree, and the name thus wrung from his jealous heart was one to live forever in the lives and legends of Siena's people.

Baroma sought the silence of his lodge, and his medicine men and braves dispersed, leaving Siena standing in the circle, a magnificent statue facing the steely north.

From that day insult was never offered to Siena, nor word spoken to him by the Crees, nor work given. He was free to come and go where he willed, and he spent his time in lessening the tasks of his people.

The trails of the forest were always open to him, as were the streets of the Cree village. If a brave met him, it was to step aside; if a squaw met him, it was to bow her head; if a chief met him, it was to face him as warriors faced warriors.

One twilight Emihiyah crossed his path, and suddenly she stood as once before, like a frail reed about to break in the wind. But Siena passed on. The days went by and each one brought less labor to Siena's people, until that one came wherein there was no task save what they set themselves. Siena's tribe were slaves, yet not slaves.

The winter wore by and the spring and the autumn, and again Siena's fame went abroad on the four winds. The Chippewayans journeyed from afar to see the Great Slave, and likewise the Blackfeet and the Yellow Knives. Honor would have been added to fame; councils called; overtures made to the somber Baroma on behalf of the Great Slave, but Siena passed to and fro among his people, silent and cold to all others, true to the place which his great foe had given him. Captive to a lesser chief, they said; the Great Slave who would yet free his tribe and gather to him a new and powerful nation.

Once in the late autumn Siena sat brooding in the twilight by Ema's tepee. That night all who came near him were silent. Again Siena was listening to voices on the wind, voices that had been still for long, which he had tried to forget. It was the north wind, and it whipped the spruces and moaned through the pines. In its cold breath it bore a message to Siena, a hint of coming winter and a call from Naza, far north of the green-white, thundering Athabasca, river without a spirit.

In the darkness when the camp slumbered Siena faced the steely north. As he looked a golden shaft, arrow-shaped and arrow-swift, shot to the zenith.

"Naza!" he whispered to the wind. "Siena watches."

Then the gleaming, changing Northern Lights painted a picture of gold and silver bars, of flushes pink as shell, of opal fire and sunset red; and it was a picture of Siena's life from the moment the rushing Athabasca rumbled his name, to the far distant time when he would say farewell to his great nation and pass forever to the retreat of the winds. God-chosen he was, and had power to read the story in the sky.

Seven nights Siena watched in the darkness; and on the seventh night, when the golden flare and silver shafts faded in the north, he passed from tepee to tepee, awakening his people. "When Siena's people hear the sound of the shooting stick let them cry greatly: 'Siena kills Baroma! Siena kills Baroma!'"

With noiseless stride Siena went among the wigwams and along the lanes until he reached Baroma's lodge. Entering in the dark he groped with his hands upward to a moose's antlers and found the shooting stick. Outside he fired it into the air.

Like a lightning bolt the report ripped asunder the silence, and the echoes clapped and reclapped from the cliffs. Sharp on the dying echoes Siena bellowed his war whoop, and it was the second time in a hundred years for foes to hear that terrible, long-drawn cry.

Then followed the shrill yells of Siena's people: "Siena kills Baroma ... Siena kills Baroma ... Siena kills Baroma!"

The slumber of the Crees awoke to a babel of many voices; it rose hoarsely on the night air, swelled hideously into a deafening roar that shook the earth.

In this din of confusion and terror when the Crees were lamenting the supposed death of Baroma and screaming in each other's ears, "The Great Slave takes his freedom!" Siena ran to his people and, pointing to the north, drove them before him.

Single file, like a long line of flitting specters, they passed out of the fields into the forest. Siena kept close on their trail, ever looking backward, and ready with the shooting stick.

The roar of the stricken Crees softened in his ears and at last died away.

Under the black canopy of whispering leaves, over the gray, mist-shrouded muskeg flats, around the glimmering reed-bordered ponds, Siena drove his people.

All night Siena hurried them northward and with every stride his heart beat higher. Only he was troubled by a sound like the voice that came to him on the wind.

But the wind was now blowing in his face, and the sound appeared to be at his back. It followed on his trail as had the step of destiny. When he strained his ears he could not hear it, yet when he had gone on swiftly, persuaded it was only fancy, then the voice that was not a voice came haunting him.

In the gray dawn Siena halted on the far side of a gray flat and peered through the mists on his back trail. Something moved out among the shadows, a gray shape that crept slowly, uttering a mournful cry.

"Siena is trailed by a wolf," muttered the chief.

Yet he waited, and saw that the wolf was an Indian. He raised the fatal shooting stick.

As the Indian staggered forward, Siena recognized the robe of silver fox and marten, his gift to Emihiyah. He laughed in mockery. It was a Cree trick. Tillimanqua had led the pursuit disguised in his sister's robe. Baroma would find his son dead on the Great Slave's trail.

"Siena!" came the strange, low cry.

It was the cry that had haunted him like the voice on the wind. He leaped as a bounding deer.

OUT OF THE GRAY FOG BURNED DUSKY EYES HALF VEILED BY DUSKY HAIR—"EMIHIYAH COMES," SHE SAID. "SIENA WAITS," HE REPLIED

Out of the gray fog burned dusky eyes half-veiled by dusky hair, and little hands that he knew wavered as fluttering leaves. "Emihiyah comes," she said.

"Siena waits," he replied.

Far to the northward he led his bride and his people, far beyond the old home on the green-white, thundering Athabasca, god-forsaken river; and there, on the lonely shores of an inland sea, he fathered the Great Slave Tribe.

YAQUI

I

SUNSET—it was the hour of Yaqui's watch. Chief of a driven remnant of the once mighty tribe, he trusted no sentinel so well as himself at the end of the day's march. While his braves unpacked the tired horses, and his women prepared the evening meal, and his bronze-skinned children played in the sand, Yaqui watched the bold desert horizon.

Long years of hatred had existed between the Yaquis of upland Sonora and the Mexicans from the east. Like eagles, the Indian tribe had lived for centuries in the mountain fastnesses of the Sierra Madre, free, happy, self-sufficient. But wandering prospectors had found gold in their country and that had been the end of their peace. At first the Yaquis, wanting only the wildness and loneliness of their homes, moved farther and farther back from the ever-encroaching advance of the gold diggers. At last, driven from the mountains into the desert, they realized that gold was the doom of their tribe and they began to fight for their land. Bitter and bloody were the battles; and from father to son this wild, free, proud race bequeathed a terrible hatred.

Yaqui was one of the last great chiefs of his once great tribe. All his life he remembered the words of his father and his grandfather—that the Yaquis must find an unknown and impenetrable hiding place or perish from the earth. When Mexican soldiers at the decree of their government made war upon this tribe, killing those who resisted and making slaves of the captured, Yaqui with his family and followers set out upon a last journey across the Sonoran wilderness. Hateful and fearful of the east, whence this blight of gold diggers and land robbers appeared to come, he had fled toward the setting sun into a waste of desert land unknown to his people—a desert of scorching heat and burning sand and tearing cactus and treacherous lava, where water and wood and grass seemed days apart. Some of the youngest children had died on the way and all except the strong braves were wearing out.

ALONE ON A RIDGE OF RISING GROUND YAQUI FACED
THE BACK TRAIL AND WATCHED WITH FALCON EYES

Alone, on a ridge of rising ground, Yaqui faced the back trail and watched with falcon eyes. Miles distant though that horizon was, those desert eyes could have made out horses against the clear sky. He did not gaze steadily, for the Indian method was to flash a look across the spaces, from near to far, and to fix the eye momentarily, to strain the vision and magnify all objects, then to avert the gaze from that direction and presently flash it back again.

Lonely, wild, and grand, the scene seemed one of lifelessness. Only the sun lived, still hot, as it burned red-gold far away on the rugged rim of this desert world. Nothing breathed in that vastness. To Yaqui's ear the silence was music. The red sun slipped down and the desert changed. The golden floor of sand and rock shaded cold to the horizon and above that the sky lost its rose, turning to intense luminous blue. In the far distance the peaks dimmed and vanished in purple. The fire of the western heavens paled and died, and over all the rock-ribbed, sand-encumbered plateau stole a wondrous gray shade. Yaqui watched until that gray changed to black and the horizon line was lost in night. Safe now from pursuers were he and his people until the dawn.

Then, guided by a speck of camp-fire light, he returned to his silent men and moaning women and a scant meal that he divided. Hunger was naught to Yaqui, nor thirst. Four days could he travel the desert without drink, an endurance most of his hardy tribe were trained to. And as for toil, the strength of his giant frame had never reached its limit. But strong chief that he was, when he listened to the moaning women and gazed at the silent, set faces of the children under the starlight he sagged to the sands and, bowing his head, prayed to his gods. He prayed for little—only life, freedom, loneliness, a hidden niche where his people would hear no steps and fear no specters on their trail. Then with unquenchable faith he stretched his great length on the sands; and the night was as a moment.

In the gray of a dawn cold, pure, and silent, with the radiant morning star shining like a silver moon, the long file of Yaquis rode and tramped westward, on down the rugged bare slopes of this unknown desert.

And out of the relentless east, land of enemies, rose the glaring sun. Like magic the frost melted off the rocks and the cool freshness of morning changed to a fiery breath. The sun climbed, and the leagues were as long as the hours. Down into a broad region of lava toiled the fugitives. Travel over the jagged crusts and through the poison-spiked cholla lamed the horses and made walking imperative. Yaqui drove his people before him, and some of the weakest fell by the way.

Out of the hot lava and stinging cactus the Indians toiled and entered a region of bare stone, cut by wind and water into labyrinthine passages where, even if they had left tracks on the hard rocks, few pursuers could have followed them. Yaqui told this to his people, told them he saw sheep on the peaks above and smelled water, and thus urged them on and on league after league toward distant purple heights. Vast and hard as had been the desert behind them, this strange upflung desert before them seemed vaster and grimmer. The trackless way led ever upward by winding passages and gorges—a gloomy and weird region of colored stone. And over all reigned the terrible merciless sun.

Yaqui sacrificed horses to the thirst and hunger of his people and abandoned the horror of toil under the sun to a slower progress by night. Blanched and magnified under the great stars, the iron-bound desert of riven rock, so unreal and weird, brought forth a chant from the lips of Yaqui's women. His braves, stoic like himself, endured and plodded on, lightening burdens of the weaker and eventually carrying the children. That night passed and a day of stupor in the shade of sun-heated rock; another night led the fugitives onward and upward through a maze of shattered cliffs, black and wild. Day dawned once more, showing Yaqui by the pitiless light that only his men could endure much more of this dragging on.

He made camp there and encouraged his people by a faith that had come to him during the night—a whisper from the spirit of his forefathers—to endure, to live, to go to a beautiful end his vision could not see. Then Yaqui stalked alone off into the fastnesses of the rocks and prayed to his gods for guidance. All about him were silence, desolation, a gray barren world of rock, a black barren world of lava. Far as his falcon eye could see to the north and east and south stretched the illimitable glaring desert, rough, peaked, spiked, riven, ghastly with yellow slopes, bleak with its bare belts, terrible with its fluted and upflung plateaus, stone faced by endless ramparts and fast bound to the fading distance. From the west, up over the dark and forlorn heights, Yaqui heard the whispers of his dead forefathers.

Another dawn found Yaqui on the great heights with the sunrise at his back and with another and more promising world at his feet.

"Land of our forefathers!" he cried out sonorously to his people, gazing mutely down into the promised land. A vast gray-green valley yawned at their feet. Leagues of grassy, rock-ribbed, and tree-dotted slopes led down to a gleaming white stream, winding like a silver ribbon down the valley, to lose itself far in the lower country, where the colored desert merged into an immense and boundless void of hazy blue—the sea.

"Great Water, where the sun sleeps," said Yaqui with long arm outstretched. "Yaqui's father's father saw it."

Yaqui carried the boy and led the way down from the heights. Mountain sheep and wild horses and deer and quail that had never before seen man showed no fear of this invasion of their wild home. And Yaqui's people, footsore and starved, gazed round them and, in the seeming safety of this desert-locked valley with its grass and water and wood and abundant game, they took hope again and saw their prayers answered and happiness once more possible. New life flushed their veins. The long slopes, ever greener as they descended, were welcome to aching eyes so tired of the glaring expanses of the desert.

For an encampment Yaqui chose the head of the valley. Wide and gently sloping, with a rock-walled spring that was the source of the stream, and large ironwood trees and pines and paloverdes, this lonely hidden spot satisfied the longing in Yaqui's heart. Almost his joy was complete. But never could he feel wholly secure again, even had he wings of an eagle. For Yaqui's keen eyes had seen gold in the sands of the stream; and gold spelled the doom of the Indian. Still Yaqui was grateful and content. Not soon indeed would his people be tracked to this fastness, and perhaps never. He cautioned his braves to save their scant gun ammunition, sending them out with bows and arrows to kill the tame deer and antelope. The weary squaws no longer chanted the melancholy songs of their woe. The long travel had ended. They unpacked their stores under the wide-spreading pines, made fires to roast the meat that would soon be brought, and attended to the ailments of the few children left to them. Soon the naked little ones, starved and cut and worn as they were, took to the clear cool water like goslings learning to swim.

Yaqui, carrying his rifle, stalked abroad to learn more of this wonderful valley. Stretching at length along the stream, he drank deeply, as an Indian who loved mountain water. The glint of gold in the wet sand did not please him as had the sweetness of the cold water. Grasping up a handful of sand and pebbles, he rubbed and washed it in his palm. Tiny grains of gold and little nuggets of gold! Somewhere up at the head of this valley lay the mother lode from which the gold had washed down.

Yaqui knew that here was treasure for which the white men would spill blood and sell their souls. But to the Indians—the Papagos, the Yumas, the man-eating Seris, and especially to the Yaquis—gold was no more than rock or sand, except that they hated it for the curse of white hunters it lured to the desert. Yaqui had found many a rich vein and ledge and placer of gold. He had hated them, and now more than any other he hated this new discovery. It would be a constant peril to his people. In times of flood this mountain stream would carry grains of gold as far as it flowed down on the desert. Yaqui saw in it a menace. But there was hope in the fact that many treasures of the desert heights would never be seen by white men. His father had told him that. This gray valley was high, cradled in the rocky uplands, and it might be inaccessible from below.

Yaqui set out to see. His stride was that of the strongest and tallest of his tribe, and distance meant little to him. Hunger gnawed at his vitals, but the long march across the wastes and heights had not tired him. Yaqui had never known exhaustion. Before the sun stood straight overhead he had ascertained that this valley of promise was shut off from the west and that the stream failed in impassable desert. From north and east he had traveled, and therefore felt a grim security. But to the south he turned apprehensive eyes. Long he tramped and high he climbed, at last to see that the valley, this land of his forefathers, could be gained from the south. Range and ridge sloped gradually to a barren desolate land of sun and cacti, far as his desert eyes could see. That must be the land of the Seris, the man-eaters. But it was a waterless hell in summer. No fear from the south till the winter rains fell! Yaqui returned to his camp, reaching there at sunset. There was joy in the dusky welcoming eyes of his young wife as she placed fresh meat before him.

"Yaqui's only son will live," she said, and pointed to the frail boy as he slept. The chief gazed somberly at the little brown face of his son, the last of his race.

Days passed. With rest and food and water the gloomy spirit of the Yaquis underwent a gradual change. The wild valley was an Indian's happy hunting ground, encompassed by lofty heights known only to sheep and eagles. Like wild animals, all savages, in the peace and loneliness of a secluded region, soon forgot past trials and fears. Still, the chief Yaqui did not forget, but as time passed and nothing disturbed the serenity of this hiding place his vigilance slowly relaxed. The wind and the sun and the solitude and the presence of antelope and wild horses always within sight of camp—these factors of primitive nature had a healing effect upon his sore heart. In the canyons he found graves and bones of his progenitors.

Days passed into weeks. The scarlet blossoms flamed at the long ends of the *ocatilla*; one morning the pale vordes, which had been bare and shiny green, appeared to have burst into full bloom, a yellow flowering that absorbed the sunlight; cacti opened great buds of magenta; from the canyon walls, on inaccessible ledges, hung the exquisite and rare desert flowers, *lluvia d'oro*, shower of gold; and many beautiful flowers lifted their faces out of the tall grasses. This magic of spring did not last long. The flowers faded, died, and blew away on the dry wind; the tall grasses slowly yellowed and bleached. Summer came. The glaring sun blazed over the eastern ramparts, burned white down over the still solemn valley, and sank like a huge ball of fire into the distant hazy sea. With the torrid heat of desert Sonora came a sense of absolute security to the chief Yaqui. His new home was locked in the furnace of the sun-blasted waste land. The clear spring of mountain water sank lower and lower, yet it did not fail. The birds and beasts that visited the valley attested to the nature of the surrounding country. So the time came when Yaqui forgot the strange feeling of distant steps upon his trail.

When autumn came all the valley was dry and gray and withered, except the green line along the stream and the perennial freshness of the cactus plants and the everlasting green of the paloverdes. With the winter season came the rains, and a wave of ever-brightening green flushed the vast valley from its eastern height of slope to the far distant mouth, where it opened into the barren breaks of the desert.

Manifestly the god of the Yaquis had not forgotten them. As the months passed child after child was born to the women of the tribe. Yaqui's dusky-eyed wife bore him a healthy girl baby. As the chief balanced the tiny brown form in his great hand he remembered speech of his own father's: "Son, let the Yaquis go back to the mountains of the setting sun—to a land free from white men and gold and fire water, to the desert valley where deer graze with horses. There let the Yaquis multiply into a great people or perish from the earth."

Yaqui watched his girl baby with a gleam of troubled hope lighting in his face. His father had spoken prophecy. There waved the green grass of the broad valley, dotted with wild horses, antelope, and deer grazing among his stock. Here in his hand lay another child—a woman child—and he had believed his son to be the last of his race. It was not too late. The god of the Indian was good. His branch of the Yaquis would mother and father a great people. But even as he fondled his babe the toe of his moccasin stirred grains of gold in the sand.

Love of life lulled Yaqui back into his dreams. To live, to have his people round him, to see his dusky-eyed wife at her work, to watch the little naked children playing in the grass, to look out over that rolling, endless green valley, so wild, so lonely, so fertile—such a proof of god in the desert—to feel the hot sun and the sweet wind and the cool night, to linger on the heights watching, listening, feeling, to stalk the keen-eyed mountain sheep, to eat fresh meat and drink pure water, to rest through the solemn still noons and sleep away the silent melancholy nights, to enjoy the games of his forefathers—wild games of riding and running—to steal off alone into the desert and endure heat, thirst, cold, dust, starvation while he sought the Indian gods hidden in the rocks, to be free of the white man whom he recognized as a superior and a baser being—to live like the eagles—to live— Yaqui asked no more.

Yaqui laid the baby back in the cradle of its mother's breast and stalked out as a chief to inspire his people.

In that high altitude the morning air was cold, exhilarating, sweet to breathe and wonderful to send the blood racing. Some winter mornings there was just a touch of frost on the leaves. The sunshine was welcome, the day was short, the night was long. Yaqui's people reverted to their old order of happy primitive life before the white man had come with greed for gold and lust to kill.

The day dawned in which Yaqui took his son out and put him upon a horse. As horsemen the Yaquis excelled all other Indian tribes of the Southwest. Boys were given lessons at an early age and taught to ride bareback. Thus as youths they developed exceeding skill and strength.

Some of the braves had rounded up a band of wild horses and had driven them into a rough rock-walled triangle, a natural trap, the opening of which they had closed with a rude fence. On this morning the Yaquis all assembled to see the wild horses broken. Yaqui, as an inspiration to his little son and to the other boys of the tribe, chose the vicious leader of the band as the horse he would first ride and break. High on the rocky wall perched the black-eyed boys, eager and restless, excited and wondering, some of them naked and all of them stretching out tousled black heads with shining ragged hair flying in the wind. The women and girls of the tribe occupied another position along the outcropping of gray wall, their colorful garments lending contrast to the scene.

The inclosure was wide and long, containing both level and uneven ground, some of which was grass and some sand and rock. A few ironwood trees and one huge paloverde, under which Indians were lolling, afforded shade. At the edge of the highest slope began a line of pine trees that reached up to the bare gray heights.

Yaqui had his braves drive the vicious leader of the wild horses out into the open. It was a stallion, of ungainly shape and rusty color, no longer young. With ugly head high, nostrils distended, mouth open and ears up, showing the white of vicious, fiery eyes, it pranced in the middle of the circle drawn by its captors.

Yaqui advanced with his long leather *riata*, and, once clear of the ring of horsemen inclosing the stallion, he waved them back. Then as the wild steed plunged to and fro, seeking for an opening in that circle, Yaqui swung the long noose. He missed twice. The third cast caught its mark, the snarling nose of this savage horse. Yaqui hauled the lasso taut. Then with snort of fright the stallion lunged and reared, pawing the air. Yaqui, hauling hand over hand, pulled him down and approached him at the same time. Shuddering all over, breathing with hard snorts, the stallion faced his captor one moment, as if ready to fight. But fear predominated. He leaped away. At the end of that leap, so powerful was the strain on him, he went down in the sand. Up he sprang, wilder than ever, and dashed forward, dragging the Indian, gaining yards of the lasso. But the mounted Yaquis blocked his passage; he had to swerve; and as he ran desperately in a circle once more the giant chief hauled hand over hand on the rope. Suddenly Yaqui bounded in and with a tremendous leap, like the leap of a huge panther, he gained the back of the stallion and seemed to become fixed there. He dropped the lasso, and with the first startled jump of the stallion the noose loosened and slipped off. Except for Yaqui's great, long brown legs, with their strung bands of muscle set like steel, the stallion was free.

The stallion bolted for the open. Only the rock wall checked his headlong flight. Then he wheeled and ran along the wall, bounding over rocks and ditches, stretching out until, with magnificent stride, he was running at his topmost speed. Along one wall and then the other he dashed, round and round and across, until the moment came when panic succeeded to fury, and then his tremendous energies were directed to the displacement of his rider. Wildly he pitched. With head down, legs stiff, feet together, he plunged over the sand, plowing up the dust, and bounding straight up. But he could not unseat his inexorable rider. Yaqui's legs banded his belly and were as steel.

Then the stallion, now lashed into white lather of sweat and froth, lunged high to paw the air and scream and plunge down to pitch again. His motions soon lost their energy, though not their fury. Then he reached back with eyes of fire and open mouth to bite. Yaqui's huge fist met him, first on the right, then, as he turned, on the left. Last he plunged to his knees and with rumbling heave of anger he fell on his side, meaning to roll over his rider. But the Yaqui's leg on that side flashed high while his hands twisted hard in the long mane. When the foiled horse rose again Yaqui rose with him, again fixed tight on his back. Another dash and burst of running, wild and blind this time and plainly losing speed, showed the weakening of the stallion. And the time arrived when, spent and beaten, he fell in the sand.

"Let Yaqui's son learn to ride like his father," said the chief to his gleeful, worshiping son.

Then the chief again stalked forth, drawn irresistibly by something in the hour.

"Let Yaqui's son watch and remember to tell his son's son," he said.

He scattered his riders to block the few passages out of the valley and he ordered his son and all the women of the tribe and their children again to climb high on the rocks, there to watch. The Indian gods said this day marked the rejuvenation of their tribe. Let his son, who would be chief some day, and his people, see the great runner of the Yaquis.

Naked except for his moccasins, the giant chief broke into a slow trot that was habitual with him when alone on a trail; and he crossed the stream and the plots of sand, and headed out into the grassy valley where deer grazed with the horses. Yaqui selected the one that appeared largest and strongest of the herd and to it he called in a loud voice, meant as well for the spirit of his forefathers and for his gods, watching and listening from the heights: "Yaqui runs to kill!"

The sleek gray deer left off their grazing and stood at gaze, with long ears erect. Then they bounded off. Yaqui broke from his trot into a long, swinging lope and the length of his stride was such that he seemed to fly over the ground. Up the valley the deer scattered and Yaqui ran in the trail of the one to which he had called. Half a mile off it halted to look back. Then it grazed a little, but soon lifted its head to look again. Yaqui ran on at the same easy, distance-devouring stride. Presently the deer dashed away and kept on until it was a mere speck in Yaqui's eyes. It climbed a deer trail that led over the heights, to be turned back there by one of Yaqui's braves. Then it crossed the wide valley to be turned back by insurmountable cliffs. Yaqui kept it in sight and watched it trot and stop, run and walk and stop again, all the way up the long grassy slope toward the head of the valley.

Here among rocks and trees Yaqui lost sight of his quarry, but he trailed it with scarcely a slackening of his pace. At length, coming out upon a level open bench, he saw the deer he had chosen to run to death. It was looking back.

Down the grassy middle of the vast valley, clear to the mouth where the stream tumbled off into space, across the wide level from slope to slope, back under the beetling heights, Yaqui pursued the doomed deer.

Leagues and leagues of fleet running had availed the deer nothing. It could not shake off the man. More and more the distance between them lessened. Terror now added to the gradual exhaustion of the four-footed creature, designed by Nature to escape its foes. Yaqui, perfect in all the primal attributes of man, was its superior. The race was not to the swift but to the enduring.

Within sight of his people and his little son Yaqui overtook the staggering deer and broke its neck with his naked hands. Then for an instant he stood erect over his fallen quarry, a tall and gaunt giant, bathed in the weird after-glow of sunset; and he lifted a long arm to the heights, as if calling upon his spirits there to gaze down upon the victory of the red man.

II

IT WAS toward evening of another day, all the hours of which had haunted Yaqui with a nameless oppression. Like a deer that scented a faint strange taint on the pure air Yaqui pointed his sensitive nose toward the east, whence came the soft wind.

Suddenly his strong vision quivered to the movement of distant objects on the southern slope. Halting, he fixed his gaze. Long line of moving dots! Neither deer nor sheep nor antelope traveled in that formation. The objects were men. Yaqui's magnified sight caught the glint of sunset red on shining guns. Mexican soldiers! That nameless haunting fear of the south, long lulled, now had its fulfillment.

Yaqui leaped with gigantic bounds down the slope. Like an antelope he sprang over rocks and dips, and once on the grassy downs he ran the swiftest race of his life. His piercing yells warned his people in time to save them from being surprised by the soldiers. The first shots of combat were fired as he hurdled the several courses of the stream. Yaqui saw the running and crawling forms of men in dusty blue—saw them aim short carbines—saw spurts of flame and puffs of smoke.

Yaqui's last few bounds carried him into the stone-walled encampment, and the whistling bullets that missed him told how the line of soldiers was spreading to surround the place. Yaqui flung himself behind the wall and crawled to where his braves knelt with guns and bows ready. Some of them were shooting. The women and children were huddled somewhere out of sight. Steel-jacketed bullets cracked on the rocks and whined away. Yaqui knew how poor was the marksmanship of the Mexicans; nevertheless it seemed to him they were shooting high. The position of the Indians was open to fire from several angles.

During a lull in the firing a hoarse yell pealed out. Yaqui knew Spanish. "Surrender, Yaquis!" was the command. The Yaquis answered by well-aimed bullets that brought sharp cries from the soldiers. Soon the encampment appeared entirely surrounded. Reports came from all sides and bullets whistled high, spatting into the trees. Then occurred another lull in the firing. Again a voice pealed out: "Surrender, Yaquis, save your lives!"

The Indians recognized their doom. Each man had only a few shells for his gun. Many had only bows and arrows. They would be shot like wolves in a trap. But no Yaqui spoke a word.

Nevertheless, when darkness put an end to their shooting there were only a few who had a shell left. The Mexicans grasped the situation and grew bold. They built fires off under the trees. They crept down to the walls and threw stones into the encampment and yelled derisively: "Yaqui dogs!" They kept up a desultory shooting from all sides as if to make known to the Indians that they were surrounded and vigilantly watched.

At dawn the Mexicans began another heavy volleying, firing into the encampment without aim but with deadly intent. Then, yelling their racial hatred of the Yaquis, they charged the camp. It was an unequal battle. Outnumbered and without ammunition the Yaquis fought a desperate but losing fight. One by one they were set upon by several, sometimes by half a dozen, Mexicans and killed or beaten into insensibility.

Yaqui formed the center of several storms of conflict. With clubbed rifle he was like a giant fighting down a horde of little men.

"Kill the big devil!" cried a soldier.

From the thick of that mêlée sounded Spanish curses and maledictions and dull thuds and groans as well. The Yaqui was a match for all that could surround him. A Mexican fired a pistol. Then the officer came running to knock aside the weapon. He shouted to his men to capture the Yaqui chief. The Mexicans pressed closer, dodging the sweeping rifle, and one of them plunged at the heels of the Indian. Another did likewise and they tripped up the giant, who was then piled upon by a number of cursing soldiers. Like a mad bull Yaqui heaved and tossed, but to no avail. He was overpowered and bound with a lasso, and tied upright to the paloverde under which he had so often rested.

His capture ended the battle. And the Mexicans began to run about, searching. Daylight had come. From under a ledge of rock the Indian women and children were driven. One lithe, quick boy eluded the soldiers. He slipped out of their hands and ran. As he looked back over his shoulder his dark face shone wildly. It was Yaqui's son. Like a deer he ran, not heeding the stern calls to halt. "Shoot!" ordered the officer. Then the soldiers leveled rifles and began to fire. Puffs of dust struck up behind, beside and beyond that flying form. But none hit him. They shot at him until he appeared to be out of range. And all eyes watched him flee. Then a last bullet struck its flying mark. The watchers heard a shrill cry of agony and saw the lad fall.

All the Indians were tied hand and foot and herded into a small space and guarded as if they had been wild cattle.

After several hours of resting and feasting and celebrating what manifestly was regarded as a great victory, the officer ordered the capture of horses and the burning of effects not transportable. Soon the beautiful encampment of the Yaquis was a scene of blackened and smoking ruin. Then, driving the Yaquis in a herd before them, the Mexicans, most of them now mounted on Indian horses, faced the ascent of the slope by which they had entered the valley.

Far down that ragged mountain slope the Mexicans halted at the camp they had left when they made their attack on the Yaquis. Mules and burros, packsaddles and camp duffel occupied a dusty bench upon which there grew a scant vegetation. All round were black slopes of ragged lava and patches of glistening white cholla.

The Yaquis received but little water and food, no blankets to sleep on, no rest from tight bonds, no bandaging of their fly-tormented wounds. But they bore their ills as if they had none.

Yaqui sat with his back to a stone and when unobserved by the guards he would whisper to those of his people nearest to him. Impassively but with intent faces they listened. His words had some strange, powerful, sustaining effect. And all the time his inscrutable gaze swept down off the lava heights to the hazy blue gulf of the sea.

Dawn disclosed the fact that two of the Yaquis were badly wounded and could not be driven to make a start. Perhaps they meant to force the death that awaited them farther down the trail; perhaps they were absorbed in the morbid gloom of pain and departing strength. At last the officer, weary of his subordinate's failure to stir these men, dragged at them himself, kicked and beat them, cursing the while. "Yaqui dogs! You go to the henequen fields!"

The older of these wounded Indians, a man of lofty stature and mien, suddenly arose. Swiftly his brown arm flashed. He grasped a billet of wood from a packsaddle and struck the officer down. The blow lacked force. It was evident that the Yaqui, for all his magnificent spirit, could scarcely stand. Excitedly the soldiers yelled, and some brandished weapons. The officer staggered to his feet, livid and furious, snarling like a dog, and ordering his men to hold back, he drew a pistol to kill the Yaqui. The scorn, the contempt, the serenity of the Indian, instead of rousing his respect, incurred a fury which demanded more than death.

"You shall walk the cholla torture!" he shrieked, waving his pistol in the air.

In northwest Mexico, for longer than the oldest inhabitant could remember, there had been a notorious rumor of the cholla torture that the Yaquis meted out to their Mexican captives. This cholla torture consisted of ripping the skin off the soles of Mexicans' feet and driving them to walk upon the cactus beds until they died.

The two wounded Indians, with bleeding raw feet, were dragged to the cholla torture. They walked the white, glistening, needle-spiked beds of cholla blind to the cruel jeers and mute wonderment and vile maledictions of their hereditary foes. The giant Yaqui who had struck down the officer stalked unaided across the beds of dry cholla. The cones cracked like live bits of steel. They collected on the Yaqui's feet until he was lifting pads of cactus. He walked erect, with a quivering of all the muscles of his naked bronze body, and his dark face was set in a terrible hardness of scorn for his murderers.

Then when the mass of cactus cones adhering to the Yaqui's feet grew so heavy that he became anchored in his tracks the Mexican officer, with a fury that was not all hate, ordered his soldiers to dispatch these two Indians, who were beyond the reach of a torture hideous and appalling to all Mexicans. Yaqui, the chief, looked on inscrutably, towering above the bowed heads of his women.

This execution sobered the soldiers. Not only extermination did they mean to mete out to the Yaqui, but an extermination of horrible toil, by which the Mexicans were to profit.

Montes, a Brazilian, lolled in the shady spot on the dock. The hot sun of Yucatan was more than enough for him. The still air reeked with a hot pungent odor of henequen. Montes had learned to hate the smell. He was in Yucatan on a mission for the Brazilian government and also as an agent to study the sisal product—an advantageous business for him, to which he had devoted himself with enthusiasm and energy.

But two unforeseen circumstances had disturbed him of late and rendered less happy his devotion to his tasks. His vanity had been piqued, his pride had been hurt, his heart had been stormed by one of Mérida's coquettish beauties. And the plight of the poor Yaqui Indians, slaves in the henequen fields, had so roused his compassion that he had neglected his work.

So, as Montes idled there in the shade, with his legs dangling over the dock, a time came in his reflection when he was confronted with a choice between the longing to go home and a strange desire to stay. He gazed out into the gulf. The gunboat *Esperanza* had come to anchor in the roads off Progreso. She had a cargo of human freight—Yaqui Indian prisoners from the wild plateaus of Northern Sonora—more slaves to be broken in the terrible henequen fields. At that moment of Montes's indecision he espied Lieutenant Perez coming down the dock at the head of a file of *rurales*.

Gazing at Perez intently, the Brazilian experienced a slight cold shock of decision. He would prolong his stay in Yucatan. Strange was the nameless something that haunted him. Jealous curiosity, he called it, bitterly. Perez had the favor of the proud mother of Señorita Dolores Mendoza, the coquettish beauty who had smiled upon Montes. She cared no more for Perez than she cared for him or any of the young bloods of Merida. But she would marry Perez.

Montes rose and stepped out of the shade. His commission in Yucatan put him on common ground with Perez, but he had always felt looked down upon by this little Yucatecan.

"Buenos dias, señor," replied Perez to his greeting. "More Yaquis."

A barge was made fast to the end of the dock and the Yaquis driven off and held there in a closely guarded group.

The time came when Perez halted the loading of henequen long enough to allow the prisoners to march up the dock between files of *rurales*. They passed under the shadows of the huge warehouses, out into a glaring square where the bare sand radiated veils of heat.

At an order from Perez, soldiers began separating the Yaqui women and children from the men. They were formed in two lines. Then Perez went among them, pointing out one, then another.

Montes suddenly grasped the significance of this scene and it had strange effect upon him. Yaqui father and son—husband and wife—mother and child did not yet realize that here they were to be parted—that this separation was forever. Then one young woman, tall, with striking dark face, beautiful with the grace of some wild creature, instinctively divined the truth and she cried out hoarsely. The silence, the stoicism of these Indians seemed broken.

This woman had a baby in her arms. Running across the aisle of sand, she faced a huge Yaqui and cried aloud in poignant broken speech. This giant was her husband and the father of that dusky-eyed baby. He spoke, laid a hand on her and stepped out. Perez, who had been at the other end of the aisle, saw the movement and strode toward them.

"Back, Yaqui dogs!" he yelled stridently, and he flashed his bright sword.

With tremendous stride the Yaqui reached Perez and towered over him.

"*Capitan*, let my wife and child go where Yaqui goes," demanded the Indian in deep voice of sonorous dignity. His Spanish was well spoken. His bearing was that of a chief. He asked what seemed his right, even of a ruthless enemy.

But Perez saw nothing but affront to his authority. At his order the *rurales* clubbed Yaqui back into his squad. They would have done the same for the stricken wife, had she not backed away from their threatening advances. She had time for a long agonized look into the terrible face of her husband. Then she was driven away in one squad and he was left in the other.

Montes thought he would forever carry in memory the tragic face of that Yaqui's wife. Indians had hearts and souls the same as white people. It was a ridiculous and extraordinary and base thing to be callous to the truth. Montes had spent not a little time in the pampas among the Gauchos and for that bold race he had admiration and respect. Indeed, coming to think about it, the Gauchos resembled these Yaquis. Montes took the trouble to go among English and American acquaintances he had made in Progreso, and learned more about this oppressed tribe.

The vast plateau of northwestern Mexico, a desert and mountainous region rich in minerals, was the home of the Yaquis. For more than one hundred and sixty years there had been war between the Yaquis and the Mexicans. And recently, following a bloody raid credited to the Yaquis, the government that happened to be in power determined to exterminate them. To that end it was hunting the Indians down, killing those who resisted capture, and sending the rest to the torture of the henequen fields.

But more interesting was the new information that Montes gathered. The Yaquis were an extraordinary, able-bodied, and intelligent people. Most of them spoke Spanish. They had many aboriginal customs and beliefs, but some were Roman Catholics. The braves made better miners and laborers than white men. Moreover, they possessed singular mechanical gifts and quickly learned to operate machines more efficiently than most whites. They possessed wonderful physical development and a marvelous endurance. At sixty years Yaquis had perfectly sound white teeth and hair as black as night.

These desert men could travel seventy miles on foot in one day with only a bag of pinole. Water they could do without for days. And it was said that some of the Yaqui runners performed feats of speed, strength, and endurance beyond credence. Montes, remembering the seven-foot stature of that Yaqui chief and the spread of shoulders and the wonder of his spare lithe limbs, thought that he could believe much.

The act of Perez in deliberately parting the chief from his loved ones was cruel and despicable; and it seemed to establish in Montes's mind an excuse for the disgust and hate he had come to feel for the tyrannical little officer. But, being frank with himself, Montes confessed that this act had only fixed a hate he already had acquired.

The Brazilian convinced himself that he had intuitively grasped a portent apparently lost on Perez. One of those silent, intent-faced Yaquis was going to kill this epauleted scion of a rich Yucatecan house. Montes had read it in these faces. He had lived among the blood-spilling Gauchos and he knew the menace of silent fierce savages. And he did not make any bones about the admission to himself that he hoped some Yaqui would kill the peacocked Mexican. Montes had Spanish in him, and something of the raw passion of the Gauchos he admired; and it suited him to absorb this morbid presentiment. The Yaqui chief fascinated him, impelled him. Montes determined to learn where this giant had been sent and to watch him, win his confidence, if such a thing was possible. *Quién sabe?* Montes felt more reasons than one for his desire to get under the skin of this big Yaqui.

III

IN THE interior of Yucatan there were vast barren areas of land fit only for the production of henequen. Nothing but jungle and henequen would grow there. It was a limestone country. The soil could not absorb water. It soaked through. Here and there, miles apart, were *cenotes*, underground caverns full of water, and usually these marked the location of a hacienda of one of the rich planters. The climate was hot, humid, and for any people used to high altitudes it spelled death.

The plantation of Don Sancho Perez, father of the young lieutenant, consisted of fifty thousand acres. It adjoined the hundred-thousand-acre tract of Donna Isabel Mendoza. The old Don was ambitious to merge the plantations into one, so that he could dominate the fiber output of that region. To this end he had long sought to win for his son the hand of Donna Isabel's beautiful daughter.

The big Yaqui Indian who had been wantonly separated from his wife by young Perez was in the squad of prisoners that had been picked out by the young officer to work on his father's plantation.

They were manacled at night and herded like wild beasts into a pen and watched by armed guards. They were routed out at dawn and put to work in the fiber fields. For food they had, each of them, a single lump of coarse soggy bread—one lump once every day. When the weaker among them began to lag, to slow down, to sicken, they were whipped to their tasks.[1]

Yaqui knew that never again would he see his wife and baby—never hear from them—never know what became of them. He was worked like a galley slave, all the harder because of his great strength and endurance. He would be driven until he broke down.

Yaqui's work consisted of cutting henequen fiber leaves. He had a curved machete and he walked down the endless aisles between the lines of great century plants and from each plant he cut the lower circle of leaves. Each plant gave him a heavy load and he carried it to the nearest one of the hand-car tracks that crossed the plantation. The work of other Indians was to push hand cars along these tracks and gather the loads.

YAQUI KNEW THAT NEVER AGAIN WOULD HE SEE HIS WIFE AND BABY—NEVER HEAR FROM THEM—NEVER KNOW WHAT BECAME OF THEM

It took Yaqui six days to cut along the length of one aisle. And as far as he could see stretched a vast, hot, green wilderness with its never-ending lines and lanes, its labyrinthine maze of intersecting aisles, its hazy, copper-hued horizons speared and spiked by the great bayonet-like leaves. He had been born and raised on the rugged mountain plateaus far to the north, where the clear, sweet, cold morning air stung and the midday sun was only warm to his back, where there were grass and water and flowers and trees, where the purple canyons yawned and the black peaks searched the sky. Here he was chained in the thick, hot, moist night, where the air was foul, and driven out in the long day under a fiery sun, where the henequen reeked and his breath clogged in his throat and his eyes were burning balls and his bare feet were like rotting hoofs.

The time came when Montes saw that the Yaqui looked no more toward that northland which he would never see again. He dreamed no more hopeless dreams. Somehow he knew when his wife and baby were no more a part of him on the earth. For something within him died and there were strange, silent voices at his elbow. He listened to them. And in the depths of his being there boiled a maelstrom of blood. He worked on and waited.

At night in the close-crowded filthy pen, with the dampness of tropical dews stealing in, and all about him the silent prostrate forms of his stricken people, he lay awake and waited enduringly through the long hours till a fitful sleep came to him. By day in the henequen fields, with the furnace blasts of wind swirling down the aisles, with the moans of his beaten and failing comrades full in his ears, he waited with a Yaqui's patience.

He saw his people beaten and scourged and starved. He saw them sicken and fail—wilt under the hot sun—die in the henequen aisles—and be thrown like dogs into ditches with quicklime. One by one they went and when they were nearly all gone another squad took their places. The Yaqui recognized Indians of other tribes of his race. But they did not know him. He had greatly changed. Only the shell of him was left. And that seemed unbreakable, deathless. He did not tell these newcomers to the fields what torture lay in store for them. He might have been dumb. He only waited, adding day by day, in the horror of the last throes of his old comrades, something more to that hell in his blood. He watched them die and then the beginning of the end for his new comrades. They were doomed. They were to be driven till they dropped. And others would be brought to fill their places, till at last there were no Yaquis left. The sun was setting for his race.

The Yaqui and his fellow toilers had one day of rest—the Sabbath. There was no freedom. And always there were guards and soldiers. Sunday was the day of bull fights in the great corral at the hacienda. And on these occasions Yaqui was given extra work. Montes knew the Indian looked forward to this day. The old Don's son, Lieutenant Perez, would come down from the city to attend the fight. Then surely Yaqui fed his dark soul with more cunning, more patience, more promise.

It was the Yaqui's work to help drag disemboweled and dying horses from the bull ring and to return with sand to cover up the gory spots in the arena. Often Montes saw him look up at the crowded circle of seats and at the box where the gray old Don and his people and friends watched the spectacle. There were handsome women with white lace over their heads and in whose dark and slumberous eyes lurked something the Yaqui knew. It was something that was in the race. Lieutenant Perez was there leaning toward the proud señorita. The Indian watched her with strange intensity. She appeared indifferent to the efforts of the *picadores* and the *banderilleros*, those men in the arena whose duty it was to infuriate the bull for the artist with the sword—the matador. When he appeared the beautiful señorita wakened to interest. But not until there was blood on the bright blade did she show the fire and passion of her nature. It was sight of blood that quickened her. It was death, then, that she wanted to see.

And last the Yaqui let his gaze rivet on the dark, arrogant visage of young Perez. Did not the great chief then become superhuman, or was it only Montes's morbid fancy? When Yaqui turned away, did he not feel a promise of fulfillment in the red haze of the afternoon sun, in the red tinge of the stained sand, in the red and dripping tongue of the tortured bull? Montes knew the Yaqui only needed to live long enough and there would be something. And death seemed aloof from this Indian. The ferocity of the desert was in him and its incalculable force of life. In his eyes had burned a seared memory of the violent thrust with which Perez had driven his wife and baby forever from his sight.

Montes's changed attitude evidently found favor in the proud señorita's eyes. She had but trifled with an earnest and humble suitor; to the advances of a man, bold, ardent, strange, with something unfathomable in his wooing, she was not indifferent. The fact did not cool Montes's passion, but it changed him somehow. The Spanish in him was the part that so ardently loved and hated; his mother had been French, and from her he had inherited qualities that kept him eternally in conflict with his instincts.

Montes had his living quarters in Mérida, where all the rich henequen planters had town houses. It was not a long horseback ride out to the haciendas of the two families in which Montes had become most interested. His habit of late, after returning from a visit to the henequen fields, had been to choose the early warm hours of the afternoon to call upon Señorita Mendoza. There had been a time when his calls had been formally received by the Donna Isabel, but of late she had persisted in her siesta, leaving Montes to Dolores.

Montes had grasped the significance of this —the future of Dolores had been settled and there no longer was risk in leaving her alone. But Montes had developed a theory that the future of any young woman was an uncertainty.

The Mendoza town house stood in the outskirts of fashionable Mérida. The streets were white, the houses were white, the native Mayan women wore white, and always it seemed to Montes as he took the familiar walk that the white sun blazed down on an immaculate city. But there were dark records against the purity of Mérida and the Yaqui slave driving was one of them. The Mendoza mansion had been built with money coming from the henequen fields. It stood high on a knoll, a stately white structure looking down upon a formal garden, where white pillars and statues gleamed among green palms and bowers of red roses. At the entrance, on each side of the wide flagstone walk, stood a huge henequen plant.

On this day the family was in town and Montes expected that the señorita would see him coming. He derived pleasure from the assurance that, compared with Perez, he was someone good to look at. Beside him the officer was a swarthy undersized youth. But Montes failed to see the white figure of the girl and suffered chagrin for his vanity.

The day was warm. As he climbed the high, wide stone steps his brow grew moist and an oppression weighed upon him. Only in the very early morning here in Yucatan did he ever have any energy. The climate was enervating. No wonder it was that servants and people slept away the warmer hours. Crossing the broad stone court and the spacious outside hall, Montes entered the dim, dark, musty parlors and passed through to the patio.

Here all was colorful luxuriance of grass and flower and palm, great still ferns and trailing vines. It was not cool, but shady and moist. Only a soft spray of falling water and a humming of bees disturbed the deep silence. The place seemed drowned in sweet fragrance, rich and subtle, thickening the air so that it was difficult to breathe. In a bower roofed by roses lay Señorita Mendoza, asleep in a hammock.

Softly Montes made his way to her side and stood looking down at her. As a picture, as something feminine, beautiful and young and soft and fresh and alluring, asleep and therefore sincere, she seemed all that was desirable. Dolores Mendoza was an unusual type for a Yucatecan of Spanish descent. She was blond. Her hair was not golden, yet nearly so; she had a broad, low, beautiful brow, with level eyebrows, and the effect of her closed lids was fascinating with their promise; her nose was small, straight, piquant, with delicate nostrils that showed they could quiver and dilate; her mouth, the best feature of her beauty, was as red as the roses that drooped over her, and its short curved upper lip seemed full, sweet, sensuous. She had the oval face of her class, but fair, not olive-skinned, and her chin, though it did not detract from her charms, was far from being strong. Perhaps her greatest attraction, seen thus in the slumber of abandon, was her slender form, round-limbed and graceful.

Montes gazed at her until he felt a bitterness of revolt against the deceit of Nature. She gladdened all the senses of man. But somehow she seemed false to the effect she created. If he watched her long in this beautiful guise of sleep he would deaden his intelligence. She was not for him. So he pulled a red rose and pushed it against her lips, playfully tapping them until she awoke. Her eyes unclosed. They were a surprise. They should have been blue, but they were tawny. Sleepy, dreamy, wonderful cat eyes they were, clear and soft, windows of the truth of her nature. Montes suddenly felt safe again, sure of himself.

"Ah, Señor Montes," she said. "You found me asleep. How long have you been here?"

"A long time, I think," he replied, as he seated himself on a bench near her hammock. "Watching you asleep, I forgot time. But alas! time flies—and you awoke."

Dolores laughed. She had perfect white teeth that looked made to bite and enjoy biting. Her smile added to her charm.

"Sir, one would think you liked me best asleep."

"I do. You are always beautiful, Dolores. But when you are asleep you seem sincere. Now you are—Dolores Mendoza."

"Who is sincere? You are not," she retorted. "I don't know you any more. You seem to try to make me dissatisfied with myself."

"So you ought to be."

"Why? Because I cannot run away with you to Brazil?"

"No. Because you look like an angel but are not one. Because your beauty, your charm, your sweetness deceive men. You seem the incarnation of love and joy."

"Ah!" she cried, stretching out her round arms and drawing a deep breath that swelled her white neck. "You are jealous. But I am happy. I have what I want. I am young and I enjoy. I love to be admired. I love to be loved. I love jewels, gowns, all I have, pleasure, excitement, music, flowers. I love to eat. I love to be idle, lazy, dreamy. I love to sleep. And you, horrid man, awake me to make me think."

"That is impossible, Dolores," he replied. "You cannot think."

"My mind works pretty well. But I'll admit I'm a little animal—a tawny-eyed cat. So, Montes, you must stroke me the right way or I will scratch."

"Well, I'd rather you scratched," said Montes. "A man likes a woman who loves him tenderly and passionately one moment and tears his hair out the next."

"You know, of course, señor," she replied mockingly. "The little Alva girl, for instance. You admired her. Perhaps she—"

"She is adorable," he returned complacently. "I go to her for consolation."

Dolores made a sharp passionate gesture, a contrast to her usual languorous movements. Into the sleepy, tawny eyes shot a dilating fire.

"Have you made love to her?" she demanded.

"Dolores, do you imagine any man could resist that girl?" he rejoined.

"Have you?" she repeated with heaving breast.

Montes discarded his tantalizing lightness. "No, Dolores, I have not. I have lived in a torment lately. My love for you seems turning to hate."

"No!" she cried, extending her hands. She softened. Her lips parted. If there were depths in her, Montes had sounded them.

"Dolores, tell me the truth," he said, taking her hands. "You have never been true."

"I am true to my family. They chose Perez for me to marry—before I ever knew you. It is settled. I shall marry him. But—"

"But! Dolores, you love me?"

She drooped her head. "Yes, señor—lately it has come to that. Ah! Don't—don't! Montes, I beg of you! You forget—I'm engaged to Perez."

Montes released her. In her confession and resistance there was proof of his injustice. She was no nobler than her class. She was a butterfly in her fancies, a little cat in her greedy joy of physical life. But in her agitation he saw a deeper spirit.

"Dolores, if I had come first—before Perez—would you have given yourself to me?" he asked.

"Ah, señor, with all my heart!" she replied softly.

"Dearest—I think I must ask you to forgive me for—for something I can't confess. And now tell me—this reception given to-morrow by your mother—is that to announce your engagement to Perez?"

"Yes and I will be free then till fall—when—when—"

"When you will be married?"

She bowed assent and hesitatingly slid a white hand toward him.

"Fall! It's a long time. Dolores, I must go back to Brazil."

"Ah, señor, that will kill me! Stay!" she entreated.

"But it would be dangerous. Perez dislikes me. I hate him. Something terrible might come of it."

"That is his risk. I have consented to marry him. I will do my duty before and after. But I see no reason why I may not have a little happiness—of my own—until that day comes. Life for me will not contain all I could wish. I told you; now I am happy. But you were included. Señor, if you love me you will remain."

"Dolores, can you think we will not suffer more?" he asked.

"I know we will afterward. But we shall not now."

"Now is perilous to me. To realize you love me! I did not think you capable of it. Listen! Something—something might prevent your marriage—or happen afterward. All—all is so uncertain."

"*Quién sabe?*" she whispered; and to the tawny, sleepy languor of her eyes there came a fancy, a dream, a mystic hope.

"Dolores, if Perez were lost to you—one way or another—would you marry me?" he broke out huskily. Not until then had he asked her hand in marriage.

"If such forlorn hope will make you stay—make you happy—yes, Señor Montes," was her answer.

There came a time when Yaqui was needed in the factory where the henequen fiber was extracted from the leaves. He had come to be a valuable machine—an instrument of toil that did not run down or go wrong. One guard said to another: "That big black peon takes a lot of killing!" and then ceased to watch him closely. He might have escaped. He might have crossed the miles and miles of henequen fields to the jungle, and under that dense cover had made his way northward to the coast. Yaqui had many a chance. But he never looked toward the north.

At first they put him to feeding henequen leaves into the maw of a crushing machine. The juicy, sticky, odorous substance of the big twenty-pound leaf was squeezed into a pulp, out of which came the white glistening threads of fiber. These fibers made sisal rope—rope second in quality only to the manila.

By and by he was promoted. They put him in the pressing room to work on the ponderous iron press which was used to make the henequen bales. This machine was a high, strange-looking object, oblong in shape, like a box, opening in the middle from the top down. It had several distinct movements, all operated by levers. Long bundles of henequen were carried in from the racks and laid in the press until it was half full. Then a lever was pulled, the machine closed on the fiber and opened again. This operation was repeated again and again. Then it was necessary for the operator to step from his platform upon the fiber in the machine and stamp it down and jump upon it and press it closely all round. When this had been done the last time the machine seemed wide open and stuffed so full that it would never close. But when the lever was pulled the ponderous steel jaws shut closer and closer and locked. Then the sides fell away, to disclose a great smooth bale of henequen ready for shipment.

The Yaqui learned to operate this press so skillfully that the work was left to him. When his carriers went out to the racks for more fiber he was left alone in the room.

Some strange relation sprang up between Yaqui and his fiber press. For him it never failed to operate. He knew to a strand just how much fiber made a perfect bale. And he became so accurate that his bales were never weighed. They came out glistening, white, perfect to the pound. There was a strange affinity between this massive, steel-jawed engine and something that lived in the Yaqui's heart, implacable and immutable, appalling in its strength to wait, in its power to crush.

IV

THERE seemed no failing of the endurance of this primitive giant, but his great frame had wasted away until it was a mere hulk. Owing to his value now to the hacienda, Yaqui was given rations in lieu of the ball of soggy bread; they were not, however, what the Indian needed. Montes at last won Yaqui's gratitude.

"Señor, if Yaqui wanted to eat it would be meat he needed," said the chief. Then Montes added meat to the wine, bread, and fruit he secretly brought to the Indian.

When Montes began covert kindnesses to the poor Yaqui slaves the chief showed gratitude and pathos: "Señor Montes is good—but the sun of the Yaquis is setting."

Perez in his triumphant arrogance evidently derived pleasure from being magnanimous to the man he instinctively knew was his rival.

One day at the hacienda when Montes rode up to meet Donna Isabel and Dolores he found them accompanied by Perez and his parents. Almost immediately the young officer suggested gayly:

"Señor, pray carry Dolores off somewhere. My father has something to plan with Donna Isabel. It must be a secret from Dolores. Take her a walk—talk to her, señor—keep her excited—make love to her!"

"I shall be happy to obey. Will you come, señorita?" said Montes.

If they expected Dolores to pout, they were mistaken. Her slow, sleepy glance left the face of her future husband as she turned away silently to accompany Montes. They walked along the palm-shaded road, out toward the huge, open, sunny space that was the henequen domain.

"I hate Perez," she burst out suddenly. "He meant to taunt you. He thinks I am his slave—a creature without mind or heart. Señor, make love to me!"

"You will be his slave—soon," whispered Montes bitterly.

"Never!" she exclaimed passionately.

They reached the end of the shady road. The mill was silent. Montes saw the Indian standing motionless close at hand, in the shade of the henequen racks.

"Dolores, did you mean what you just said?" asked Montes eagerly.

"That I will never be Perez's slave?"

"No; the other thing you said."

"Yes, I did," she replied. "Make love to me, señor. It was his wish. I must learn to obey."

With sullen scorn she spoke, not looking at Montes, scarcely realizing the actual purport of her speech. But when Montes took her in his arms she started back with a cry. He held her. And suddenly clasping her tightly he bent his head to kiss the red lips she opened to protest.

"Let me go!" she begged wildly. "Oh—I did not—mean—Montes, not so! Do not make me—"

"Kiss me!" whispered Montes hoarsely, "or I'll never let you go. It was his wish. Come, I dare you—I beg you!"

One wild moment she responded to his kiss, and then she thrust him away.

"Ah, by the saints!" she murmured with hands over her face. "Now I will love you more—my heart will break."

"Dolores, I can't let Perez have you," declared Montes miserably.

"Too late, my dear. I am to be his wife."

"But you love me, Dolores?"

"Alas! too true. I do. Oh, I never knew how well!" she cried.

"Let us run away," he implored eagerly.

Mournfully she shook her head, and looking up suddenly she espied the Yaqui. His great burning cavernous eyes, like black fire, were fixed upon her.

"Oh, that terrible Yaqui," she whispered. "It is he who watches us at the bull fights—Let us go, Montes—Oh, he saw us—he saw me—Come!"

Upon their return to the house the old Don greeted them effusively. He seemed radiant with happiness. He had united two of the first families of Yucatan, which unison would make the greatest henequen plantation. The beautiful señorita had other admirers. But this marriage had unusual advantages. The peculiar location and productiveness of the plantations and the obstacles to greater and quicker output that would be done away with, and the fact that Lieutenant Perez through his military influence could work the fields with peon labor—these facts had carried the balance in favor of the marriage. The old Don manifestly regarded the arrangement as a victory for him which he owed to the henequen, and he had decided to make the wedding day one on which the rich product of the plantation should play a most important part.

"But how to bring in the henequen!" he concluded in perplexity. "I've racked my brain. Son, I leave it to you."

Young Perez magnificently waved the question aside. Possessing himself of his fiancée's reluctant hand, he spoke in a whisper audible to Montes. "We planned the wedding presents. That was the secret. But you shall not see—not know—until we are married!"

Montes dropped his eyes and his brow knit thoughtfully. Later, as a peon brought his horse, he called Perez aside.

"I've an idea," he said confidentially. "Have Yaqui select the most perfect henequen fiber to make the most beautiful and perfect bale of henequen ever pressed. Have Yaqui place the wedding presents inside the bale before the final pressing. Then send it to Donna Isabel's house after the wedding and open it there."

Young Perez clapped his hands in delight. What a capital plan! He complimented Montes and thanked him and asked him to keep secret the idea. Indeed, the young lieutenant waxed enthusiastic over the plan. It would be unique; it would be fitting to the occasion. Perez would have Yaqui pick over and select from the racks the most perfect fibers, to be laid aside. Perez would go himself to watch Yaqui at his work. He would have Yaqui practice the operation of pressing, so at the momentous hour there could be no hitch. And on the wedding day Perez would carry the presents himself. No hands but his own would be trusted with those jewels, especially the exquisite pearls that were his own particular gift.

At last the day arrived for the wedding. It was to be a holiday. Yaqui alone was not to lie idle. It was to fall to him to press that bale of henequen and to haul it to the bride's home.

But Perez did not receive all his gifts when he wanted them. Messengers arrived late and some were yet to come. He went to the mill, however, and put Yaqui to work at packing the henequen in the press and building it up. The Indian was bidden to go so far with the bale, leaving a great hole in the middle for the gifts and to have the rest of the fiber all ready to pack and press. Perez would not trust anyone else with his precious secret; he himself would hurry down with the gifts, and secretly, for the manner of presentation was to be a great surprise.

Blue was the sky, white gold the sun, and the breeze waved the palms. But for Montes an invisible shadow hovered over the stately Mendoza mansion where Dolores was to be made a bride. The shadow existed in his mind and took mystic shape—now a vast, copper-hazed, green-spiked plain of henequen, and then the spectral gigantic shape of a toiling man, gaunt, grim, and fire-eyed.

Montes hid his heavy heart behind smiling lips and the speech of a courtier. He steeled himself against a nameless and portending shock, waiting for it even when his mind scorned the delusion. But the shock did not come at sight of Señorita Dolores, magnificently gowned in white, beautiful, serene, imperious, with her proud, tawny eyes and proud, red lips. Nor when those sleepy strange eyes met his. Nor when the priest ended the ceremony that made her a wife.

He noted when Lieutenant Perez laughingly fought his way out of the crowd and disappeared. Then the unrest of Montes became a haunting suspense.

By and by the guests were directed out to the shaded west terrace, where in the center of the wide stoned space lay a huge white glistening bale of henequen. Beside it stood the giant Yaqui, dark, motionless, aloof. The guests clustered round.

When Montes saw the Yaqui like a statue beside the bale of henequen, he sustained the shock for which he had been waiting. He slipped to the front of the circle of guests.

"Ah!" exclaimed the old Don, eyeing the bale of henequen with great satisfaction. "This is the surprise our son had in store for us. Here is the jewel case—here are the wedding presents!"

The guests laughed and murmured their compliments.

"Where is Señor Perez?" demanded the Don as he looked round.

"The boy is hiding," replied Donna Isabel. "He wants to watch his bride when she sees the gifts."

"No—he would not be there," declared the old Don in perplexity. Something strange edged into his gladness of the moment. Suddenly he wheeled to the Yaqui. But he never spoke the question on his lips. Slowly he seemed to be blasted by those great black-fired orbs, as piercing as if they had been lightnings from hell.

"Hurry, open the bale," cried the bride, her sweet voice trilling above the gay talk.

Yaqui appeared not to hear. Was he looking into the soul of the father of Lieutenant Perez? All about him betrayed almost a superhuman intensity.

"Open the bale," ordered the bride.

Yaqui cut the wire. He did not look at her. The perfectly folded and pressed strands of fiber shook and swelled and moved apart as if in relief. And like a great white jewel case of glistening silken threads the bale of henequen opened.

It commanded a stilling of the gay murmur—a sudden silence that had a subtle effect upon all. The beautiful bride, leaning closer to look, seemed to lose the light of the tawny proud eyes. Her mother froze into a creature of stone. The old Don, in slow strange action, as if his mind had feeble sway over body, bent his gray head away from the gaunt and terrible Yaqui. Something showed blue down under the center strands of the glistening fiber. With a swift flash of his huge black hand, with exceeding violence, Yaqui swept the strands aside. Then from his lips pealed an awful cry. Instead of the jewels, there, crushed and ghastly, lay the bridegroom Perez.

TIGRE

"YES, I've a power over animals. Look at Tigre there! But the old women in Micas say I've found one wild thing I'll never tame."

"And that, *señor?*" asked Muella.

"My young and pretty wife."

She tossed her small head, so that her black curls rippled in the sunlight, and the silver rings danced in her ears.

"Bernardo, I'm not a parrot to have my tongue slit, or a monkey to be taught tricks, or a jungle cat to be trained. I'm a woman, and—"

"Yes—and I am old," he interrupted bitterly. "Look, Muella—there on the Micas trail!"

"It's only Augustine, your *vaquero.*"

"Watch him!" replied Bernardo.

Muella watched the lithe figure of a man striding swiftly along the trail. He was not going to drive cattle up to the corrals, for in that case he would have been riding a horse. He was not going toward the huts of the other herders. He faced the jungle into which ran the Micas trail.

Surely he could not be on his way to Micas! The afternoon was far advanced and the village many miles away. No *vaquero* ever trusted himself to the dangers of the jungle at night. Even Augustine, the boldest and strongest of Bernardo's many herders, would scarcely venture so much. Yet Augustine kept on down the trail, passed the thatched bamboo fence, went through the grove of palms, and disappeared in the green wall of jungle.

"He's gone!" cried Bernardo. "Muella, I sent Augustine away."

She saw a dull red in her husband's cheeks, a dark and sinister gleam in his eyes; and her surprise yielded to misgiving.

"Why?" she asked.

"He loved you."

"No! No! Bernardo, if that's why you sent him away, you've wronged him. Of all your *vaqueros*, Augustine alone never smiled at me—he cared nothing for me."

"I say he loved you," returned Bernardo hoarsely.

"Bernardo, you are unjust!"

"Would you lie to me? I know he loves you. Girl, confess that you love him. Tell it! I won't bear this doubt another day!"

Muella stood rigid in his grasp, her eyes blazing the truth that her lips scorned to speak.

"I'll make you tell!" he shouted, and ran to a cage of twisted vines and bamboo poles.

As he fumbled with the fastening of a door, his brown hands shook. A loud purr, almost a cough, came from the cage; then an enormous jaguar stepped out into the sunlight.

"Now, girl, look at Tigre!"

Tigre was of huge build, graceful in every powerful line of his yellow, black-spotted body, and beautiful. Still, he was terrible of aspect. His massive head swung lazily; his broad face had one set expression of brute ferocity.

The eyes of any jaguar are large, yellow, cold, pale, cruel, but Tigre's were frightful. Every instant they vibrated, coalesced, focused, yet seemed always to hold a luminous, far-seeing stare. It was as if Tigre was gazing beyond the jungle horizon to palm-leaf lairs which he had never seen, but which he knew by instinct. And then it was as if a film descended to hide their tawny depths. Tigre's eyes changed—they were always changing, only there was not in them the life of vision; for the jaguar was blind.

Bernardo burst into rapid speech.

"The taunting old crones of Micas were right when they said I could not tame the woman; but I've tamed every wild creature of the Taumaulipas jungle. Look at Tigre! Who beside Bernardo ever tamed a jaguar? Look! Tigre is my dog. He loves me. He follows me, he guards me, he sleeps under my hammock. Tigre is blind, and he is deaf, yet never have I trained any beast so well. Whatever I put Tigre to trail, he finds. He never loses. He trails slowly, for he is blind and deaf, but he never stops, never sleeps, till he kills!"

Bernardo clutched the fur of the great jaguar and leaned panting against the thatch wall of the cage.

"I'll soon know if you love Augustine!" he went on passionately. "Look here at the path—the path that leads out to the Micas trail. See! Augustine's sandal-prints in the dust! Now, girl, watch!"

He led Tigre to the path and forced the nose of the beast down upon Augustine's footmarks. Suddenly the jaguar lost all his lax grace. His long tail lashed from side to side. Then, with head low, he paced down the path. He crossed the grassy plot, went through the fence, along the trail into the jungle.

"He's trailing Augustine!" cried Muella.

She felt Bernardo's gaze burning into her face.

"Tigre will trail him—catch him—kill him!" her husband said.

Muella screamed.

"He's innocent! I swear Augustine does not love me! I swear I don't love him! It's a horrible mistake. He'll be trailed—ah, he'll be torn by that blind brute!" Muella leaped back from her husband. "Never! You jealous monster! For I'll run after Augustine—I'll tell him—I'll save him!"

She eluded Bernardo's fierce onslaught, and, fleet as a frightened deer, she sped down the path. She did not heed his hoarse cries, nor his heavy footsteps.

Bernardo was lame. Muella had so little fear of his catching her that she did not look back. She passed the fence, sped through the grove, and entered the jungle.

II

THE trail was hard-packed earth, and ahead it lost its white line in the green walls. Muella ran swiftly, dodging the leaning branches, bowing her head under the streamers of moss, striking aside the slender palm leaves. Gay-plumaged birds flitted before her, and a gorgeous butterfly crossed her path. A parrot screeched over her head.

She strained her gaze for the trailing jaguar. Then she saw him, a long black and yellow shape moving slowly under the hanging vines and creepers.

When Muella caught up with Tigre, she slackened her pace, and watched for a wide place in the trail where she could pass without touching him.

"I must pass him," she muttered. "He can't hear me—I can do it safely—I must!"

But still she did not take advantage of several wide places.

Presently the trail opened into a little glade. Twice she started forward, only to hang back. Then desperately she went on, seeing nothing but the great spotted cat just in front of her.

TWICE SHE STARTED FORWARD, ONLY TO HANG BACK

Sharp spear-point palm leaves stung her face, and their rustling increased her terror. She flashed by Tigre so close that she smelled him.

Muella uttered a broken cry and began to run, as if indeed she were the wild creature Bernardo had called her. She looked over her shoulder to see the sinuous yellow form disappear round a bend of the trail. Then she gathered courage. For a long time her flying feet pattered lightly on the trail. She was young, supple, strong, and it took much to tire her. She ran on and on, until her feet were heavy, her breath was almost gone, and her side pierced by a sharp pain. Then she fell to a walk, caught her breath, and once more ran.

Fears began to beset her. Had Augustine left the trail? How swiftly he had walked! It seemed as if she had run several miles. But that was well, for, the larger the distance the farther she would get ahead of the jaguar.

Shadows began to gather under the overhanging vines and creepers. Only the tips of the giant ceibas showed a glint of sunlight. The day was fast closing. Once more she ran on and on; and then, as she turned a curve, a tall, dark form stood out of the green, and blurred the trail.

"Augustine! Wait! Wait!" she cried.

The man swung round, and ran back. Muella, panting for breath and with her hand pressed over her heart, met him.

"*Señora!* What has happened?" he exclaimed.

"Wait! My breath's gone!" she gasped. "Wait! But keep on—we—we mustn't stop!"

Muella took a fleeting upward glance at him. It was so hurried that she could not be positive, but she thought she had caught a strange, paling flush of his bronzed face and a startled look of his dark eyes. Why should his meeting her unexpectedly cause more than surprise or concern?

As she trotted along, she shot another quick glance up at him. He seemed unmistakably agitated; and this disconcerted her. She heard his amazed questions, but they were mostly unintelligible.

She had thought of nothing save to catch up with him and to blurt out that Tigre was on his trail, and why. The words now halted on her lips. It was not easy to tell him. What would he say—what would he do? A few moments back, he had been only one of Bernardo's herders—the best, truly, and a man whom it was pleasing to look upon, but he had been nothing to her. He alone of the *vaqueros* had not smiled at her, and this piquing of her pride had gained him notice which otherwise he might never have got.

As she pattered on, slowly regaining her breath, the presence of the man seemed to grow more real. It was well that she knew Augustine cared nothing for her, else she could not have told him of Bernardo's unjust suspicions.

The trail opened into a clearing, where there were several old palm-thatched huts, a broken-down corral, and a water hole. The place had once been used by Bernardo's herders, but was now abandoned and partly overgrown. At this point, Augustine, who for a time had silently stalked beside Muella, abruptly halted her.

"*Señora,* what is wrong? Where are you going?"

"Going!" She uttered a little laugh. "Why, I don't know. I followed—to warn you. Bernardo put Tigre on your trail!"

"Tigre? *Santa Maria!*"

"Yes. I ran, and ran, and passed him. He must be far back now. He's slow at first, but he's sure, and he's trailing you. Hurry on! You mustn't stop here!"

"*Señora!* You ran—you risked so much to save me? Oh, may our Blessed Lady reward you!"

"Man, I tell you, don't stop. Go on! You have only your machete. Why did you start into the jungle without a gun?"

"Bernardo drove me off. I owned nothing at the hacienda except my blanket and machete."

"He's selfish—he was beside himself. Why, Augustine, he was jealous. He—he told me he drove you away because you—you cared for me. I'm ashamed to tell you. But, Augustine, he's growing old. You mustn't mind—only hurry to get safe from that terrible brute!"

"I forgive him, *señora*. It's his way to fall in a rage; but he quickly repents. And you, *señora*—you must take this old trail back to the hacienda. Go swiftly, for soon it will be night."

"I'm not going back," said Muella slowly. "I won't live any longer with Bernardo. Take me to Micas—to my sister's home!"

With one long stride Augustine barred the trail and stood over her.

"You must go back. It's best you should know the truth. Bernardo spoke truth when he told you I loved you!"

"Augustine, you're telling a lie—just to frighten me back to him!"

"No. Bernardo asked me for the truth; so I told him."

Muella's eyes dilated and darkened with shadows of amaze, wonder, and pain.

"Oh, why did you tell him? I didn't know. Oh, I swore by the Virgin that you had no thought of me. He'll believe that I lied."

"*Señora*, you are innocent, and Bernardo will learn it. You know him—how hotheaded he is, how quickly he is sorry. Go back. Take this old cattle road—here—and hurry. The sun has set. You must run. Have no fear for me!"

"I'm not going back to Bernardo." She straightened up, pale and composed, but as she stepped forward to pass the *vaquero* in the trail she averted her eyes. "Take me to Micas!"

With a passionate gesture Augustine stopped her.

"But, *señora*, consider. Darkness is upon us. Micas is a long way. You're only a girl. You can't keep up. You've forgotten that Tigre is on my trail."

"I forget nothing," she replied coldly. "I've begged you to hurry."

"Muella, go back at once. To-morrow—after a night in the jungle—with me—you can't go. It'll be too late!"

"It's too late now," breathed the girl. "I can't go back—now!"

"Go first, then," he said, whipping out the long machete. "I'll wait here for Tigre."

"*Señor*, there are other *tigres*. There are panthers, too, and wild boars. I may lose the trail. Will you let me go alone?"

III

AUGUSTINE whispered the name of a saint, and turning his dark face toward where the trail led out of the clearing, he strode on without sheathing his machete.

Muella kept close to him, and entered the enclosing walls of jungle verdure. She felt indeed that she was the untamed thing Bernardo had called her, and now she was hunted. Light as dropping leaves, her feet pattered in the trail. Augustine loomed beside her, striding swiftly, and now and then the naked blade he carried, striking against a twig or branch, broke the silence with a faint ring.

The green walls became hovering shadows and turned to gray. Muella had an irresistible desire to look back. The darkening menace of the gloom before and on each side was nothing to that known peril behind. She saw nothing, however, but a dull, gray, wavering line fading into the obscurity of the jungle. She strained her hearing. Except for the soft swishing of her skirt on the brush, and the occasional low ring of Augustine's machete, there was absolutely no sound.

She noted that her companion never turned his head. Had he no fear? Quick flashes of memory recalled stories of this herder's daring. How tall and powerful he was—how swiftly he strode—how dark and stern and silent he seemed! He must know full well the nature of Bernardo's pet, the terrible blind brute that never failed on a trail.

All at once the jungle grew into two ragged walls of black separated by a narrow strip of paler shade. Night had fallen; and with it came a blinking of stars through dense foliage overhead, and the lighting of fireflies. Insects began to hum. Rustlings in the brush augmented Muella's sensitiveness. A strange call of a night bird startled her, and instinctively she shrank closer to Augustine. She wished to speak to him, to make the silence bearable; but stealthy steps off to the right made her heart leap and her tongue mute.

Augustine heard, for he struck the leaves with his machete. From the enshrouding blackness came the snapping of twigs, pattering little steps, the rush of animals running through grass or ferns, and soft rustlings in the brush. Then the night silence awoke to strange cries—squall of cat and scream of panther, squeaks and grunts and squeals of peccaries, and inexpressibly wild sounds, too remote to distinguish.

"Oh, Augustine!" whispered Muella, fear at last unlocking her lips. "Listen! All before us—do you hear?"

"*Señora*, we have not greatly to fear ahead," he replied. "But behind—a trailing *tigre* warms with the night! We must not lag!"

"I'm not tired. I can walk so, all night; but the steps, the cries, frighten me. It grows darker, and I stumble."

She fancied she saw him reach out as if to help her, and then draw suddenly back. The darkness became so thick that she could scarcely see him. Like a tall specter he moved on.

She groped for his arm, found it, and slipped her hand down to his. Instantly she felt his strong fingers convulsively close round hers. The warm clasp helped and cheered her.

So, mile after mile, Muella kept tireless pace with the herder; and when the jungle creatures ceased their hue and quest, and the dead silence once more settled thickly down, the strange night flight lost its reality and seemed a dream. The black shadows lifted and paled to opaque gloom. A whiteness stole into the jungle; silver shafts gleamed through the trees. The moon was rising. Muella hailed it with joy, for it meant that the night was far advanced, and that their way would be lightened.

Soon all about her was a radiant, encompassing world of silver shadows and gleams. It was a beautiful night. The cold fear weighting her heart lessened, seemed momentarily to be thrilled and warmed away. She loved that great, silver-orbed, golden-circled moon; and now she looked up at it through a streaked and fringed and laced web.

She wondered if Augustine saw the beauty of the sharp-cut palms, the delicate-leaved bamboos, and the full-foliaged ceibas, all festooned with long silver streamers of moss. Gnarled branches of a dead monarch of the forest, silhouetted against the deep blue of the sky, showed orchids and aloes and long, strangling vines—parasites that had killed it. Every unshadowed leaf along the trail glistened white with dew. The glamor of the white night was upon Muella.

Augustine's voice broke the spell.

"You are tiring, but we must not lag. Shall I carry you?"

"No, no! I can keep up."

His words and the glint of his naked machete brought her back to actuality. She slipped her hand from his.

Slowly a haze overspread the moon. The brightness failed, and then the moonlit patches imperceptibly merged into the shadows, until all was gray. The jungle trees rose dim and weird and lost their tips in clouds of mist. A chicolocki burst into song, and the broken notes heralded the coming of day.

"Augustine, it is near dawn," said Muella. "Oh, how good the light will be! I'm so cold—so wet. We shall be safe in Micas soon, shall we not?"

The herder mumbled a reply that she did not understand.

IV

SWIFTLY upon the gray dawn came the broad daylight. The clouds of creamy mist rose and broke and rolled away, letting the sunshine down into the jungle. The balmy air rang with the melodies of birds. Flocks of parrots passed overhead, screeching discordant clamor.

Presently it struck Muella that the trail was growing narrow and rough and overgrown. She had journeyed to Micas often enough to be familiar with the trail, and this, so wild and crooked, was not the right one.

"Augustine, have you missed the way?" she queried anxiously.

Briefly he replied that he was making a short cut. Muella did not believe him. She walked on, and began again to look back. When she caught Augustine doing likewise, she gave way to dread.

The morning wore on, the sun grew warm, and with the heat of day came the jungle flies and mosquitoes. Augustine was inured to their attacks, but Muella impatiently fought them, thus adding to her loss of energy.

When, at the crossing of a network of trails, Augustine chose one at random, Muella was certain of the worst. She asked him about it, and he admitted he was off the course, but as he was sure of his direction there was no need of fear. He assured her that he would have her at her sister's home in Micas by noon.

Noon found them threading a matted jungle where they had to bend low along the deer and peccary trails. The character of the vegetation had changed. It was now dry, thorny, and almost impenetrable.

Suddenly Muella jerked her hand away from a swinging branch, which she had intended to brush aside.

"Look, Augustine, on my hand. Garapatas! Ugh, how I loathe them!"

Her hand and wrist were dotted with great black jungle ticks. Augustine removed them, and as he did so, Muella saw his fingers tremble. The significance of his agitation did not dawn upon her until she was free of the pests, and then she fancied that her touch had so moved him. It was wonderful, it warmed her blood, and she stole a glance at him. But Augustine was ashen pale; his thoughts were far from the softness and beauty of a woman's hand.

"Augustine! You have lost your way!" she cried.

Gloomily he dropped his head, and let his silence answer.

"Lost in the jungle! We're lost! And Tigre is on our trail!" she shrieked.

Panic overcame her. She tottered and fell against him. Her whole slender length rippled in a violent trembling. Then she beat her hands frantically on Augustine's shoulders, and clutched him tight, and besought him with inarticulate speech.

"Listen, *señora*, listen," he kept saying. "If you give up now, I can't save you. We're lost, but there's a way out. Listen—don't tear at me so—there's a way out. Do you hear? You go on alone—follow these deer tracks till you come to water. Soon they'll lead to water. That water will be the Santa Rosa. Follow up the stream till you come to Micas. It'll be hard, but you can do it."

"Go on alone! And you?" she said brokenly.

"I'll turn on our back trail. I'll meet Tigre and stop him."

"Tigre will kill you!"

"He is blind and deaf. I shall be prepared. I've a chance, at least, to cripple him."

"At the end of a trail Tigre is a demon. He has been trained to kill the thing he's put to trail. You—with only a machete! Ah, *señor*, I've heard that you are brave and strong, but you must not go back to meet Tigre. Come! We'll follow the deer tracks together. Then if Tigre catches us—well, he can kill us both!"

"*Señora*, I can serve you best by going back."

"You think that if you took me to Micas the old women would talk—that my good name would be gone?" she asked searchingly.

"*Señora*, we waste time, and time is precious," he protested.

Muella studied the haggard, set face. This man meant to sacrifice his life for her. Deep through the fire of his eyes she saw unutterable pain and passion. If she had doubted his love, she doubted no more. He must be made to believe that she had followed him, not alone to save him from Tigre, but because she loved him. Afterward he would be grateful for her deceit. And if her avowal did not break his will, then she would use a woman's charm, a woman's sweetness.

"*Señor*, you told Bernardo the truth—and I lied to him!" she said.

Stranger than all other sensations of that flight was the thrill in her as she forced herself to speak.

"What do you mean?" demanded Augustine.

"He asked you if you loved me. You told the truth. He asked me if—if I loved you. And—I lied!"

"*Santa Maria!*" the man cried, starting up impulsively. Then slowly he fell back. "*Señora*, may the saints reward you for your brave words. I know! You are trying to keep me from going back. We waste precious time—go now!"

"Augustine, wait, wait!" she cried.

Running blindly, she flung herself into his arms. She hid her face in his breast, and pressed all her slender, palpitating body close to his. As if he had been turned to stone, he stood motionless. She twined her arms about him, and her disheveled hair brushed his lips. She tried to raise her face—failed—tried again, and raised it all scarlet, with eyes close shut and tears wet on her cheeks. Blindly she sought his mouth with her lips—kissed him timidly—tremulously—and then passionately.

With that, uttering a little gasp, she swayed away and turned from him, her head bowed in shame, one beseeching hand held backward to him.

"Don't go! Don't leave me!"

"*Dios!*" whispered Augustine.

Presently he took the proffered hand, and, leading her, once more plunged into the narrow trail.

V

FOR hours Muella walked with lowered eyes. She plodded on, bending her head under the branches, and constantly using her free hand to fight the pests.

Her consciousness, for the while, was almost wholly absorbed with a feeling of an indefinable difference in herself. She seemed to be in a condition of trembling change, as if the fibers of her soul were being unknit and rewoven.

Something illusive and strange and sweet wavered before her—a promise of joy that held vague portent of pain. This inexplicable feeling reminded her of fancies, longings, dreams of her girlhood.

At length sensations from without claimed full share of Muella's attention. The heat had grown intense. She was becoming exhausted. Her body burned, and about her ankles were bands of red-hot fire. Still she toiled on, because she believed that Micas was close at hand.

The sun went down, and night approached. There was no sign of water. Augustine failed to hide his distress. He was hopelessly lost in the jungle. All the trails appeared to lead into the same place—a changeless yellow and gray jungle.

The flies pursued in humming wheel, and clouds of whining mosquitoes rose from the ground. The under side of every leaf, when brushed upward, showed a red spot which instantly disintegrated, and spilled itself like a bursting splotch of quicksilver upon the travelers. And every infinitesimal red pin point was a crawling jungle pest. The dead wood and dry branches were black with innumerable garapatas.

Muella had been born a hill native, and she was not bred to withstand the savage attack of the jungle vermin. The time came when she fell, and implored Augustine to put her out of her misery with his machete. For answer he lifted her gently and moved on, carrying her in his arms.

Night came. Augustine traveled by the stars, and tried to find trails that led him in a general direction northward. By and by Muella's head rolled heavily, and she slept.

At length the blackness and impenetrable thicket hindered his progress. He laid Muella down, covered her with his blanket, and stood over her with drawn machete till the moon rose.

The light aiding him, he found a trail, and, taking up his burden, he went on. And that night dragged to dawn.

Muella walked little the next day. She could hardly stand. She had scarcely strength to free her hair from the brush as it caught in passing. The burning pain of her skin had given place to a dull ache. She felt fever stealing into her blood.

Augustine wandered on, over bare rocks and through dense jungles, with Muella in his arms. He was tireless, dauntless, wonderful in his grim determination to save her. Worn as she was, sick and feverish, she yet had moments when she thought of him; and at each succeeding thought he seemed to grow in her impression of strength and courage.

But most of her thoughts centered on the trailing Tigre. The serpents and panthers and peccaries no longer caused Muella concern; she feared only the surely gaining jaguar.

VI

NIGHT closed down on them among tangled mats and labyrinthine webs of heavy underbrush.

"Listen!" whispered Muella suddenly, with great black eyes staring out of her white face.

From far off in the jungle came a sound that was like a cough and growl in one.

"Ah! Augustine, did you hear?"

"Yes."

"Was it a *tigre?*"

"Yes."

"A trailing *tigre?*"

"Yes, but surely that could not have been Bernardo's. His *tigre* would not give cry on a trail."

"Oh, yes. Tigre is deaf and blind, and he has been trained, but he has all the jungle nature. He has Bernardo's cruelty, too!"

Again the sound broke on the still night air. Muella slipped to the ground with a little gasp. She heard Augustine cursing against the fate that had driven them for days under trees, trees, trees, and had finally brought them to bay in a corner where there was no tree to climb. She saw him face about to the trail by which they had come; and stand there with his naked blade upraised. He blocked the dim, narrow passageway.

An interminable moment passed. Muella stopped breathing, tried to still the beating of her heart so that she could listen. There was no sound save the low, sad hum of insects and the rustle of wind in leaves. She seemed to feel Tigre's presence out there in the blackness. Dark as it was, she imagined she saw him stealing closer, his massive head low, his blind eyes flaring, his huge paws reaching out.

A slight rustling checked all motion of her blood. Tigre was there, ready to spring upon Augustine. Muella tried to warn him, but her lips were dry and dumb. Had he lost his own sense of hearing?

Her head reeled and her sight darkened; but she could not swoon. She could only wait, wait, while the slow moments wore on.

Augustine loomed over the trail, a dark, menacing figure. Again there came a rustling and a stealthy step, this time in another direction; and Augustine turned toward it.

Long silence followed; even the humming of insects and the moaning of the wind seemed to grow fainter. Then came more tickings of the brush and a padded footfall. Tigre had found them—was stalking them!

Muella lay there, helplessly waiting. In the poignancy of her fear for Augustine, expecting momentarily to see the huge jaguar leap upon him, she forgot herself. There was more in her agony of dread than the sheer primitive shrinking of the flesh, the woman's horror of seeing death inflicted. Through that terrible age-long flight through the jungle, Augustine had come to mean more than a protector to her.

She watched him guardedly facing in the direction of every soft rustle in the brush. He was a man at the end of his resources, ready to fight and die for a woman.

The insects hummed on, the wind moaned in the leaves, the rustlings came from one point and another in the brush, but Tigre did not appear. The black night lightened and the moon rose. Muella now distinctly saw Augustine— disheveled and ragged, white and stern and wild, with his curved blade bright in the moonlight.

Then the gray mist crept up to obscure the white stars and the moon, and at last the blue vault. The rustlings ceased to sound in the brush. From far off rasped the cough of a *tigre*. It appeared to come from the same place as when first heard. Hope had new birth in Muella's heart.

Moments like hours passed; the insects ceased to hum and the wind to moan. The gray shadows fled before a rosy dawn.

Augustine hewed a lane through the dense thicket that had stopped him, and presently he came upon a trail. He hurried back to Muella with words of cheer. Strength born of hope returned to her, and she essayed to get up.

Helping her to her feet, he half led and half carried her into the trail. They went on for a hundred paces, to find that the path suddenly opened into a wide clearing. To Muella it had a familiar look, and Augustine's exclamation assured her that he had seen the place before. Then she recognized a ruined corral, some old palm-thatched huts, and a water hole as belonging to the clearing through which they had long before passed.

"We've traveled back in a circle!" exclaimed Augustine. "We're near the hacienda—your home!"

Muella leaned against him and wept. First of all was the joy of deliverance.

"Muella, you are saved," Augustine went on. "The distance is short—I can carry you. Bernardo will forgive—you know how he flies into a passion, and then how he repents."

"Yes, yes. I'll go back to him—tell him the truth—ask his mercy!"

From the center of the clearing came a rustling of dry leaves, then a loud purr, almost a cough. Augustine stiffened, and Muella clutched frantically at him.

For a long moment they stood, dark eyes staring into dark eyes, waiting, listening. Then Augustine, releasing his hold on the trembling girl, cautiously stepped upon a log and peered over the low palms. Almost instantly he plunged down with arms uplifted.

"*Santa Maria!* Tigre! He's there!" he whispered. "He's there, beside the body of something he's killed. He's been there all night. He was there when we first heard him. We thought he was trailing. Muella, I must see closer. Stay back—you must not follow!"

But as he crept under the low palms she followed him. They came to the open clearing. Tigre lay across the trail, his beautiful yellow and black body stretched in lax grace, his terrible sightless eyes riveted on a dead man beside him.

"Muella—stay back—I fear—I fear!" said Augustine.

He crept yet a little farther, and returned with pale face and quivering jaw.

"Muella, it's Bernardo! He's dead—has been dead for days. When you started off that day to warn me, Bernardo must have run round by the old wagon road to head off Tigre. The blind brute killed him!"

"Bernardo repented!" moaned Muella. "He repented!"

THE RUBBER HUNTER

IQUITOS was a magnet for wanderers and a safe hiding place for men who must turn their faces from civilization. Rubber drew adventurers and criminals to this Peruvian frontier town as gold lured them to the Klondike.

Among the motley crowd of rubber hunters boarding the *Amazonas* for the up-river trip was a Spaniard, upon whom all eyes were trained. At the end of the gangplank, Captain Valdez stopped him and tried to send him back. The rubber hunter, however, appeared to be a man whom it would be impossible to turn aside.

"There's my passage," he shouted. "I'm going aboard."

No one in Iquitos knew him by any other name than Manuel. He headed the list of outlaw rubber hunters, and was suspected of being a slave hunter as well. Beyond the Andes was a government which, if it knew aught of the slave traffic, had no power on that remote frontier. Valdez and the other boat owners, however, had leagued themselves together and taken the law into their own hands, for the outlaws destroyed the rubber trees instead of tapping them, which was the legitimate work, and thus threatened to ruin the rubber industry. Moreover, the slave dealers alienated the Indians, and so made them hostile.

Captain Valdez now looked doubtfully at Manuel. The Spaniard was of unusual stature; his cavernous eyes glowed from under shaggy brows; his thin beard, never shaven, showed the hard lines of his set jaw. In that crowd of desperate men he stood out conspicuously. He had made and squandered more money than any six rubber hunters on the river; he drank *chicha* and had a passion for games of chance; he had fought and killed his men.

"I'm going aboard," he repeated, pushing past Valdez.

"One more trip, then, Manuel," said the captain slowly. "We're going to shut down on you outlaws."

"They're all outlaws. Every man who has nerve enough to go as far as the Pachitier is an outlaw. Valdez, do you think I'm a slaver?"

"You're suspected—among others," replied the captain warily.

"I never hunted slaves," bellowed Manuel, waving his brawny arms. "I never needed to sell slaves. I always found cowcha more than any man on the river."

"Manuel, I'll take you on your word. But listen—if you are ever caught with Indians, you'll get the chain gang or be sent adrift down the Amazon."

"Valdez, I'll take my last trip on those terms," returned Manuel. "I'm going far—I'll come in rich."

Soon after that the *Amazonas* cast off. She was a stern-wheeler with two decks—an old craft as rough-looking as her cargo of human freight. On the upper deck were the pilot house, the captain's quarters, and a small, first-class cabin, which was unoccupied. The twenty-four passengers on board traveled second-class, down on the lower deck. Forward it was open, and here the crew and passengers slept, some in hammocks and the rest sprawled on the floor. Then came the machinery. Wood was the fuel used, and stops were made along the river when a fresh supply was needed.

Aft was the dining saloon, a gloomy hole, narrow and about twelve feet long, with benches running on two sides. At meal times, the table was lowered from the ceiling by a crude device of ropes and pulleys.

The night of the departure this saloon was a spectacle. The little room, with its dim, smelly lamp and blue haze of smoke, seemed weirdly set between the vast reaches of the black river. The passengers crowded there, smoking, drinking, gambling. These hunters, when they got together, spoke in very loud tones, for in the primeval silence and solitude of the Amazonian wilderness they grew unaccustomed to the sound of their own voices. Many languages were spoken, but Spanish was the one that gave them general intercourse.

It was a muggy night, and the stuffy saloon reeked with the odors of tobacco and perspiration and the fumes of *chicha*. The unkempt passengers sat coatless, many of them shirtless, each one adding to the din around the gambling board.

Presently the door of the saloon was filled by the form of a powerful man. From his white face and blond hair he might have been taken for an Englishman. The several gambling groups boisterously invited him to play. He had a weary, hunted look that did not change when he began to gamble. He played indifferently, spoke seldom, and lost at every turn of the cards. There appeared to be no limit to his ill luck or to his supply of money.

Players were attracted from other groups. The game, the stakes, the din, the flow of *chicha*—all increased as the night wore on.

Like the turn of the tide, the silent man's luck changed. After nearly every play he raked in the stakes. Darker grew those dark faces about the board, and meaning glances glittered. A knife gleamed low behind the winner's back, clutched in a lean hand of one of the gamesters. Murder might have been done then, but a big arm swept the gamester off his feet and flung him out of the door, where he disappeared in the blackness.

"Fair play!" roared Manuel, his eyes glowing like phosphorus in the dark. The sudden silence let in the chug of machinery, the splashing of the paddle wheel, the swishing of water. Every eye watched the giant Spaniard. Then the game recommenced, and, under Manuel's burning eyes, continued on into the night.

At last he flipped a gold piece on the table and ordered *chicha* for all.

"Men, drink to Manuel's last trip up the river," he said. "I'm coming in rich."

"Rubber or Indians?" sarcastically queried a weasel-featured Spaniard.

"Bustos, you lie in your question," replied Manuel hotly. "You can't make a slave hunter of me. I'm after rubber. I'll bring in canoes full of rubber."

Most of the outlaws, when they could not find a profitable rubber forest, turned their energies to capturing Indian children and selling them into slavery in the Amazonian settlements.

"Manuel, where will you strike out?" asked one.

"For the headwaters of the Palcazu. Who'll go with me?"

Few rubber hunters besides Manuel had ever been beyond the junction of the Pachitea and the Ucayali; and the Palcazu headed up in the foothills of the Andes. Little was known of the river, more than that it marked the territory of the Cashibos, a mysterious tribe of cannibals. None of the men manifested a desire to become Manuel's partner. He leered scornfully at them, and cursed them for a pack of cowards.

After that night he had little to do with his fellow passengers, used tobacco sparingly, drank not at all, and retreated sullenly within himself. Manuel never went into the jungle out of condition.

The *Amazonas* turned into the Ucayali, and day and night steamed up that thousand-mile river, stopping often for fuel, and here and there to let off the rubber hunters. All of them bade Manuel good-by with a jocund finality. At La Boca, which was the mouth of the Pachitea and the end of Captain Valdez's run, there were only three passengers left of the original twenty-four—Bustos, Manuel, and the stranger who seemed to have nothing in common with the rubber hunters.

"Manuel," said Bustos, "you've heard what the Palcazu is—fatal midday sun, the death dews, the man-eating Cashibos. You'll never come in. *Adios!*"

Then Captain Valdez interrogated Manuel.

"Is it true you are going out to the Palcazu?"

"Yes, captain."

"That looks bad, Manuel. We know Indians swarm up there—the Chunchus of the Pachitea, and farther out the Cashibos. We've never heard of rubber there."

"Would I go alone into a cannibal country if I hunted slaves?"

"What you couldn't do has yet not been proven. Remember, Manuel—if we catch you with Indian children, it's the chain gang or the Amazon."

Manuel, cursing low, lifted his pack and went down the gangplank. As he stepped upon the dock a man accosted him.

"Do you still want a partner?"

The question was put by the blond passenger. Manuel looked at him keenly for the first time, discovering a man as powerfully built as himself, whose gray eyes had a shadow, and about whom there was a hint of recklessness.

"You're not a rubber hunter?" asked Manuel.

"No."

"Why do you want to go with me? You heard what kind of a country it is along the Palcazu?"

"Yes, I heard. That's why I want to go."

"Ha, ha!" laughed Manuel curiously. "*Señor*, what shall I call you?"

"It's no matter."

"Very well, it shall be *Señor*."

Manuel carried his pack to a grove of palms bordering the river, where there was a fleet of canoes. Capmas Indians lounged in the shade, waiting for such opportunity to trade as he presented. Evidently Manuel was a close trader, for the willing Indians hauled up several canoes, from which he selected one. For a canoe, its proportions were immense; it had been hollowed from the trunk of a tree, was fifty feet long, three wide, and as many deep.

"*Señor*, I'm starting," said Manuel, throwing his pack into the canoe.

"Let's be off, then," replied *Señor*.

"But—you still want to go?"

"Yes."

"I've taken out strangers to these parts—and they never came back."

"That's my chance."

"*Señor*, up the Pachitea the breeze seldom blows. It's hot. Sand flies humming all day long—mosquitoes thicker than smoke—creeping insects—spiders, snakes, crocodiles, poison dews, and fevers—and the Cashibos. If we get back at all, it will be with tons of rubber. I ask no questions. I, too, have gone into the jungle and kept my secret. *Señor*, do you go?"

Señor silently offered his hand; and these two, outlaw and wanderer, so different in blood and the fortunes of life, exchanged the look that binds men in the wilderness. Whereupon Manuel gave one of the eighteen-foot, wide-bladed paddles to his companion, and, pushing the canoe off the sand, began to pole upstream close to the bank. None but the silent Campas Indians saw their departure, and soon they, and the grove of palms, and the thatched huts disappeared behind a green bend of the river.

The Pachitea, with its smooth current, steamed under the sun. The voyagers kept close to the shady side. The method of propelling the canoe permitted only one to work at a time. Beginning at the bow, he sunk his paddle to the bottom, and, holding it firmly imbedded, he walked the length of the canoe. When he completed his walk to the stern, his companion had passed to the bow. Thus the momentum of their canoe did not slacken, and they made fast time.

Gradually the strip of shade under the full-foliaged bank receded until the sun burned down upon them. When the tangled balls of snakes melted off the branches, and the water smoked and the paddles were too hot to handle, Manuel shoved the canoe into the shade of overhanging vines. It was a time when all living things, except the heat-born sand flies, hid from the direct rays of the midday sun. While the Spaniard draped a net over the bow of the canoe these sand flies hummed by like bullets. Then Manuel motioned his comrade to crawl with him under cover, and there they slept away those hours wherein action was forbidden.

About the middle of the afternoon they awoke to resume their journey; leisurely at first, and then, as the sun declined, with more energy. Fish and crocodiles rippled the surface of the river, and innumerable wild fowl skimmed its green width.

Toward sunset Manuel beached on a sandy bank, where there was a grove of *siteka* trees. He had gone into the jungle at this point and brought out rubber. The camp site was now waist deep in vegetation, which Manuel mowed down with his machete. Then he built two fires of damp leaves and wood, so they would smoke and somewhat lessen the scourge of mosquitoes. After that he carried up the charcoal box from the canoe and cooked the evening meal.

Manuel found it good to unseal the fountain of speech, that always went dry when he was alone in the jungle. It took him a little while to realize that he did all the talking, that Señor was a silent man who replied only to a direct question, and then mostly in monosyllables. Slowly this dawned upon the voluble Spaniard, and slowly he froze into the silence natural to him in the wilderness.

They finished the meal, eating under their head nets, and then sat a while over the smoky fires, with the splash of fish and the incessant whining hum of mosquitoes in their ears. When the stars came out, lightening the ebony darkness, they manned the canoe again, and for long hours poled up the misty gloom of the river.

In the morning they resumed travel, slept through the sweltering noon, and went on in the night. At the end of the fifth day's advance, Manuel pointed out the mouth of a small tributary.

"So far I've been. Beyond here all is strange to me. White men from Lima have come down the river; but of those who have gone up farther than this, none have ever returned."

What a light flashed from the eyes of his partner! Manuel was slow to see anything singular in men. But this served to focus his mind on the strangest companion with whom he had ever traveled.

Señor was exceedingly strong and implacably tireless; a perfect fiend for action. He minded not the toil, nor the flies, nor the mosquitoes, nor the heat; nothing concerned him except standing still. Señor never lagged, never shirked his part of the labor, never stole the bigger share of food, which was more than remarkable in the partner of a rubber hunter.

So Manuel passed through stages of attention, from a vague stirring of interest to respect and admiration, and from these to wonder and liking, emotions long dormant within him. The result was for him to become absorbed in covert observation of his strange comrade.

Señor ate little, and appeared to force that. He slept only a few hours every day, and his slumbers were restless, broken by turning and mumbling. Sometimes Manuel awakened to find him pacing the canoe or along a sandy strip of shore. All the hot hours of their toil he bent his broad shoulders to the paddle, wet with sweat. Indeed, he invited the torture of the sun and flies. His white face, that Manuel likened to a woman's, was burned red and bitten black and streaked with blood.

When Manuel told him to take the gun and kill wild fowl, he reached instinctively for it with the action of a man used to sport, and then he drew back and let his companion do the shooting. He never struck at one of the thousands of snakes, or slapped at one of the millions of flies, or crushed one of the millions of flies, or one of the billions of mosquitoes.

When Manuel called to Señor, as was frequently necessary in the management of the canoe, he would start as if recalled from engrossing thought. Then he would work like an ox, so that it began to be vexatious for Manuel to find himself doing the lesser share. Slowly he realized Señor's intensity, the burning in him, the tremendous driving power that appeared to have no definite end.

For years Manuel had been wandering in wild places, and, as the men with whom he came in contact were brutal and callous, answering only to savage impulses, so the evil in him, the worst of him, had risen to meet its like. But with this man of shadowed eye Manuel felt the flux and reflux of old forces, dim shades drawn from old memories, the painful resurrection of dead good, the rising of the phantom of what had once been the best in him.

The days passed, and the Pachitea narrowed and grew swifter, and its green color took on a tinge of blue.

"A-ha!" cried Manuel. "The Palcazu is blue. We must be near the mouth. Listen."

Above the hum of the sand flies rose a rumble, like low thunder, only a long, unending roll. It was the roar of rapids. The men leaned on their paddles and trudged the length of the canoe, steadily gliding upstream, covering the interminable reaches, winding the serpentine bends. The rumble lulled and swelled, and then, as they turned a bend, burst upon their ears with clear thunder. The Palcazu entered the larger river by splitting round a rocky island. On one side tumbled a current that raced across the Pachitea to buffet a stony bluff. On the other side sloped a long incline of beautiful blue-green water, shining like painted glass.

Manuel poled up the left shore as far as possible, then leaped out to wade at the bow. Señor waded at the stern, and thus they strove against the current. It was shallow, but so swift that it made progress laboriously slow, and it climbed in thin sheets up the limbs of the travelers. Foot by foot they ascended the rapid, at last to surmount it and beach the canoe in a rocky shore.

"Water from the Andes!" exclaimed Manuel. "It's years since I felt such water. Here's a bad place to float a canoe full of rubber."

"You'll have jolly sport shooting this rapid," replied Señor.

"We're entering Cashibos country now. We must eat fish—no firing the guns."

Wild cane grew thick on the bank; groves of the white sitekas led to the dark forest where the giant capirona trees stood out, their tall trunks bare and crimson against the green; and beyond ranged densely wooded hills to far distant purple outline of mountains or clouds.

"There's cowcha here, but not enough," said Manuel.

They rested, as usual during the blistering noon hours, then faced up the Palcazu. Before them stretched a tropical scene. The blue water reflected the blue sky and the white clouds, and the hanging vines and leaning orchid-tufted, creeper-covered trees. Green parrots hung back downward from the branches, feeding on pods; macaws of gaudy plumage wheeled overhead; herons of many hues took to lumbering flight before the canoe.

The placid stretch of river gave place to a succession of rapids, up which the men had to wade. A downpour of rain joined forces with the stubborn current in hindering progress. The supplies had to be covered with palm leaves; stops had to be made to bail out the canoe; at times the rain was a blinding sheet. Then the clouds passed over and the sun shone hot. The rocks were coated with a slime so slippery that sure footing was impossible.

Manuel found hard wading; and Señor, unaccustomed to such locomotion, slid over the rocks and fell often. The air was humid and heavy, difficult to breathe; the trees smoked and the river steamed. Another chute, a mill race steep as the ingenuity of the voyagers, put them to tremendous exertions. They mounted it and rested at the head, eyes down the glancing descent.

"What jolly sport you'll have shooting that one!" exclaimed Señor; and he laughed for the first time; not mirthfully, rather with a note that rang close to envy.

Manuel gazed loweringly from under his shaggy brows. This was the second time Señor had spoken of the return trip. Manuel's sharpening wits divined a subtle import—Señor's consciousness that for himself there would be no return. The thing fixed itself on Manuel's mind and would not be shaken. Blunt and caustic as he was, something withheld his speech; he asked only himself, and knew the answer. Señor was another of those men who plunge into the unbroken fastnesses of a wild country to leave no trace. Wanderers were old comrades to Manuel. He had met them going down to the sea and treading the trails; and he knew there had been reasons why they had left the comforts of home, the haunts of men, the lips of women. Derelicts on the drifting currents had once been stately ships; wanderers in the wilds had once swung with free stride on sunny streets.

"He's only another ruined man," muttered Manuel, under his breath. "He's going to hide. After a while he will slink out of the jungle to become like all the others—like me!"

But Manuel found his mind working differently from its old habit; the bitterness that his speech expressed could not dispel a yearning which was new to him.

While making camp on a shelf of shore he was absorbed in his new thoughts, forgetting to curse the mosquitoes and ants.

When the men finished their meal, twilight had shaded to dusk. Owing to the many rapids, travel by night had become impossible. Manuel drooped over one smoky fire and Señor sat by another. After sunset there never was any real silence in the jungle. This hour was, nevertheless, remarkably quiet. It wore, shaded, blackened, into wild, lonely night. The remoteness of that spot seemed to dwell in the sultry air, in the luminous fog shrouding the river, in the moving gloom under the black trees, in the odor of decaying vegetable life.

Manuel nodded and his shoulders sagged. Presently Señor raised his head, as if startled.

"Listen!" he whispered, touching his comrade's arm.

Then in the semidarkness they listened. Señor raised his head net above his ears.

"There! Hear it?" he breathed low. "What on earth—or in hell? What is it?"

"I hear nothing," replied Manuel.

Señor straightened his tall form and stood with clenched hands.

"If that was fancy—then—" He muttered deep in his chest. All at once he swayed to one side. And became strung in the attitude of listening. "Again! Hear it! Listen!"

Out of the weird darkness wailed a soft, sad note, to be followed by another, lower, sweeter, and then another still fainter.

"I hear nothing," repeated Manuel. This time, out of curiosity and indefinable portent, he lied.

"No! You're sure?" asked Señor huskily. He placed a shaking hand on Manuel. "You heard no cry—like—like—" He drew up sharply. "Perhaps I only thought I heard something—I'm fanciful at times."

He stirred the camp fire and renewed it with dry sticks. Evidently he wanted light. A slight blaze flickered up, intensifying the somber dusk. A vampire bat wheeled in the lighted circle. Manuel watched his companion, studying the face, somehow still white through the swollen fly blotches and scorch of sun, marveling at its expression. What had Señor imagined he had heard?

Again the falling note! Clearer than the clearest bell, sweeter than the saddest music, wailed out of a succession of melancholy, descending tones, to linger mournfully, to hold the last note in exquisite suspense, to hush away, and leave its phantom echo in the charged air. A woman, dying in agony and glad to die, not from disease or violence, but from unutterable woe, might have wailed out that last note to the last beat of a broken heart.

Señor gripped Manuel's arm.

"You heard that—you heard it? Tell me!"

"Oh, is that what you meant? Surely I heard it," replied Manuel. "That's only the Perde-alma."

"Perde-alma?" echoed Señor.

"Bird of the Lost Soul. Sounded like a woman, didn't it? We rubber hunters like his song. The Indians believe he sings only when death is near. But that signifies nothing. For above the Pachitea life and death are one. Life is here, and a step there is death! Perde-alma sings seldom. I was years on the river before I heard him."

"Bird of the Lost Soul! A bird! Manuel, I did not think that cry came from any living thing."

He spoke no more, and paced to and fro in the waning camp-fire glow, oblivious to the web of mosquitoes settling on his unprotected head.

Manuel pondered over the circumstance till his sleepy mind refused to revolve another idea. In the night he awoke and knew from the feeling of his unrested body that he had not slept long. He had been awakened by his comrade talking in troubled slumber.

"Lost soul—wandering—never to return! Yes! Yes! But oh let me forget! Her face! Her voice! Could I have forgotten if I had killed her? Driven, always driven—never to find—never—"

So Señor cried aloud, and murmured low, and mumbled incoherently, till at last, when the black night wore gray, he lay silent.

"A woman!" thought Manuel. "So a woman drove him across the seas to the Palcazu. Driven—driven! How mad men are!"

Señor had turned his face from his world, to drift with the eddying stream of wanderers who follow no path and find no peace, to be forgotten, to end in evil, to die forlorn—all for a woman.

In the darkness of this Peruvian forest, Señor lay amid the crawling vermin unconsciously muttering of a woman. Night spoke aloud thoughts deep hidden by day. Señor had a sailor's eye, a soldier's mien; he had not shrunk from the racking toil, the maddening insects, the blood-boiling heat; he was both strong and brave; yet he was so haunted by a woman that he trembled to hear the fancied voice of his ghost of love in the wailing note of a jungle bird. That note was the echo of his haunting pain. Señor's secret was a woman.

Manuel understood now why he had been inexplicably drawn to this man. A ghost had risen out of his own dead years. It rolled back time for Manuel, lifting from the depths a submerged memory, that, like a long-sunken bell, rang the muffled music of its past.

Out of the gray jungle gloom glided the wraith of one he had loved long ago. She recalled sunny Spain—a grassy hill over the blue bay—love—home— dark in his inner eye. And the faint jungle murmuring resembled a voice. Thus after absence of years, Manuel's ghost of love and life had come to him again. It had its resurrection in the agony of his comrade. For Manuel there was only that intangible feeling, the sweetness of remembered pain. Life had no more shocks to deal him, he thought; that keen ache in the breastbone, that poignant pang could never again be his. Manuel was life worn. He felt an immunity from further affliction, and consciousness of age crept across the line of years.

How different from other mornings in the past was the breaking of this gray dawn! The mist was as hard to breathe, the humidity as oppressive, the sun as hot, and the singing spiteful, invisible, winged demons stung with the same teeth of poisoned fire—all the hardship of jungle travel was as before, yet it seemed immeasurably lessened.

For many years Manuel had slaved up these smoky rivers, sometimes with men who hated him, and whom he learned to hate. But no man could have hated Señor. In these enterprises of lonely peril, where men were chained together in the wilderness, with life strained to the last notch, there could be no middle course of feeling. A man must either hate his companion and want to kill him, or love him and fight to save him.

So Manuel loved Señor, and laughed at the great white wonder of it, lightening it all; and once again the sealed fountain of his speech broke and flowed. Back in the settlement *chicha* had always loosed Manuel's tongue, liberated wild mirth, incited fierce passions; here in the jungle the divining of another's pain, such as had seared him years before, pierced to the deeps of his soul, and brought forth kind words that came haltingly through lips long grimly set to curse.

In the beginning of that new kinship, Señor looked in amaze upon his changed comrade, and asked if he had fever. Manuel shook his shaggy head.

Señor then fell silent; but he listened, he had to listen, and, listening, forgot himself. A new spirit fused the relation of these men.

"Señor, we are hunters," said Manuel. "I for gold that I do not want and shall easily find, you for—"

"Peace, Manuel, peace, that I ceaselessly want, but will never find."

Onward the voyagers poled and waded up the blue Palcazu. The broken waters held them to five miles a day. Only giants could have made even so many. The slimy rocks over which floundered the hydra-headed balls of snakes, the stench of hot ponds behind the bars, the rush of current to be fought inch by inch, the torrents of rain, the bailing of the canoe, the merciless heat, and the everwhirling, steel-colored bands of venomous flies—these made day a hell, rest a time of pain, sleep a nightmare; but the hunters, one grim, the other gay, strengthened with the slow advance.

Often Manuel climbed the banks, to return saying there was cowcha, more than he had seen, yet still not enough. They must go higher, to richer soil. They camped where sunset overtook them. As they sat over the smoky fires or fished in the river or lay side by side under the tent, Manuel talked. He had gone over the vast fund of his wilderness knowledge, experience in that sun-festered world, stories of river and jungle, of fights and fevers. Circling back on his seafaring life, as castaway, mariner, smuggler, he dredged memory of the happenings of those years till he reached the catastrophe that had made him a wanderer.

"What made me a caucho outlaw?" he queried, whipping his big hand through the flying swarm about his face. "A woman! What sends most wandering men down the false trails of the world? What drove you, comrade? Perhaps a woman! *Quien sabe?* I loved a girl. She had eyes like night—lips of fire—she was as sweet as life. See my hand tremble! Señor, it was years ago—five, maybe ten, I don't remember—what are years? We were married, and had a cottage on a grassy hill above the bay, where the wind blew, and we could see the white ripples creeping up the sand. Then a sailor came from over the sea; a naval man, Señor, of your country. He had seen the world; he could fascinate women—and women change their love. She walked with me along the beach in the twilight. The wind tossed her hair. I repeated gossip, accused her of loving this man I had never seen. She acknowledged her love; proudly, I thought bravely; surely without shame. Señor, with these same hands I forced her to her knees, stifled her cry—and slowly, slowly watched the great staring eyes grow fixed and awful—the lips fall wide—"

"You strangled her?" burst from Señor in passionate force.

"I was a fiend," went on the Spaniard. "I felt nothing except that her love had changed. I fled over the seas. For long my mind was dark, but clearness came, and with it truth. How I knew it I can't say—these things abide in mystery—but my girl was innocent. Then hell gaped for me. Burning days—endless nights under the hateful stars—no rest—her last cry, like the Perde-alma, Señor—her great, wide eyes—the beat, the beat, the eternal beat of pain, made him you see a thing of iron and stone.

"What was left, Señor? Only a wild life. You see the wanderer with crimes on him thick as his gray hairs. Ah! What I might have done—might have been! I see that in your eyes. What a man might have been! Holy Mercy! A braver part no man ever had chance to play. I could have left her free. I would not have heard the hound of remorse ever baying my trail. I could have hidden like a stricken deer, and died alone. But I was a blind coward. Men see differently after years go by. What is love? What is this thing that makes one woman all of life to a man? Constant or fickle, she is fair to him. Bound or free, she answers to nameless force."

"Where did you—all this happen?" asked Señor hurriedly and low.

"It was at Malaga, on the Mediterranean."

Señor stalked off into the gloom, whispering.

Manuel did not notice his comrade's agitation; he was in the rude grip of unfamiliar emotions. His story had been a deliberate lie, yet it contained truth enough to recall the old feeling out of its grave. He thought he had divined Señor's secret, his sacrifice, the motive behind his wandering in a God-forsaken land. He believed it was to leave a woman free and to forget. He felt the man's burning regret that he had not spilled blood in vengeance. So he had lied, had made himself a murderer, that by a somber contrast Señor might see in forgiveness and mercy the nobler part.

Deep in Manuel's bitter soul he knew how he had lied—for that woman of his youth had not been innocent; he had not harmed her, and he had left her free. Señor would believe his fabricated tragedy, and, looking on this hulk of a man, this wandering wretch, haunted by what he might have been, and, thanking God for his clean hands, might yet see the darkness illumined.

More days the hunters poled and pulled up the Palcazu, to enter, at length, the mouth of a deep estuary coming in from the north.

This water was a blue-green reflection of sky and foliage. It was a beautiful lane, winding between laced and fringed, woven and flowered walls. The heavy perfume of overluxuriance was sickening. Life was manifold. The estuary dimpled and swelled and splashed—everywhere were movements and sounds of water creatures. Gorgeous parrots screeched from the trailing vines; monkeys chattered from the swishing branches. Myriads of bright-plumaged birds, flitting from bank to bank, gave the effect of a many-colored net stretched above the water. Dreamy music seemed to soar in the rich, thick atmosphere.

The estuary widened presently into a narrow, oval lake, with a sandy shore on the north. Crocodiles basked in the sun, and, as Manuel turned the canoe shoreward, they raised themselves on stumpy legs, jaws wide, grotesque and hideous, and lunged for the water.

"Cayman! I never saw so many," exclaimed Manuel, striking right and left with his paddle. "Where I find caymans, there's always cowcha. Señor, I believe here is the place."

They ascended the bank, and threaded a maze of wild cane rising to higher ground. The soil was a rich alluvial. Manuel dug into it with his hands, as if, indeed, he expected to find gold there. The ridge they mounted was not thickly forested. Manuel made two discoveries—they were on the borderland of the eastern Andes, and all about them were rubber trees. Whether or not Manuel cared for the fortune represented by one hundredth part of the rubber he could see, certain it was that he ran from one tree to another clasping each in a kind of ecstasy.

"Iquitos will go mad," he cried. "A thousand tons of cowcha in sight! It's here. Look at the trees—fifty, sixty feet high! Señor, we shall go in rich, rich, rich!"

They packed the supplies up from the river to escape the sand flies, and built a shack, elevating it slightly on forked sticks to evade the marching ants and creeping insects. Inside the palm-leaf walls they hung the net, fitting it snugly in the cramped space. By clearing away the underbrush and burning the ground bare, they added still more to the utility of their camp site, and, as far as it was possible in that jungle, approached comfort.

A troop of monkeys took refuge in the tops of some palms and set up a resentful chattering; parrots and macaws swelled the unwelcoming chorus; a boa wound away from the spot, shaking a long line of bushes; and an anteater ran off into the *sitekas*.

Manuel caught up his gun, making as if to pursue the beast, then slowly laid the weapon down.

"I'd forgotten. We're in Cashibos country now. I've seen no signs, but we had best be quiet. At that we may have to shoot the jaguars. They stalk a man."

The rubber hunters worked from dawn till the noonday heat, rested through the white, intense hours, resumed their tasks in the afternoon, and continued while the light lasted. The method of honest rubber hunters was to tap a tree in the evening and visit it the next morning to get the juice. This was too slow a process for Manuel—as it took several days for a flow of a few ounces.

He was possessed with exceeding skill in the construction of clay vessels to catch the milky juice and in extracting rubber. He carried water from the river and fashioned large clay repositories, one for so many rubber trees; also he made small vessels and troughs. These baked hard in the sun. Then he cut the trees so the sap would flow freely. They would die; but that was of no moment to the outlaw. He had brought a number of kettles, in which he made a thick steam by heating palm nuts. Taking a stick with a clay mold on the end, he dipped it first in the milk, and then dried the milk in the stream. From a vessel full of milk, he got one third its weight in rubber.

"Señor," he said proudly, "I can make a hundred pounds of rubber in a day."

It was a toil-filled time, in which the united efforts of Manuel and Señor were given to making an immense cargo of rubber. Swiftly the days passed into weeks, the weeks summed months, and the rainy season was at hand. Soon the rubber hunters must expect a daily deluge, a flooded, sticky forest, intolerable humidity, and sun like an open furnace door.

Manuel awoke from his lust for rubber.

"The canoe won't hold another layer," he said. "She'll be loggy enough now. We can rest and drift clear to Iquitos. How good! We must be starting."

Like a flitting shadow, a strange, sad smile crossed Señor's face. Its meaning haunted Manuel, and recalled the early days of the trip, before the craze for rubber had driven all else from his mind. A wonderful change had come over Señor. He gave all his strength to the gathering of rubber, but no longer with a madness for sheer action. He no longer invited the torture of the stinging pests. He ate like a hungry man, and his sleep was untroubled. Even his silence had undergone change. The inward burning, the intensity of mind forever riveted upon the thing that had been the dividing spear of his life, had given place to austere tranquillity.

Other enlightenment flashed into Manuel's darksome thought. The fancy grew upon him that he had come to be to Señor what Señor was to him. He sensed it, felt it, finally realized it.

Pondering this man's deep influence, he tried to judge what it meant. Something shook his pulse, some power from without; some warm, living thing drew him to Señor. It was more than the intimate bond of men of like caliber, alone in the wilds, facing peril carelessly, dependent upon one another. Too subtle it was for Manuel, too mysterious for his crude reasoning; always it kept aloof, in the fringe of his mind. He floundered in thought, and seemed to go wandering in the realms of imagery, to become lost in memory, where the unreal present mingled with the actual past, through both of which ran Señor's baffling, intangible hold on his heartstrings.

"Maybe I've got a touch of fever," he soliloquized.

Another day went by, and still he hesitated to speak the word for departure. More and more the task grew harder, for added watching, thought, realization, strengthened his conviction that Señor intended to remain alone on the Palcazu. Had the man come to hide in the jungle, to face his soul in the solitude, to forget in the extremes of endurance? Yes, but more! He sought the end—annihilation!

Manuel had never feared to use his tongue, yet now he could not speak. It was midday, and he lay beside Señor in the shack, sheltered from the torrid heat. Usually absolute silence prevailed at this hour. On this day, however, gentle gusts of wind beat the fronds of the palms. What a peculiar sound! It had no similarity to the muffled beating of the heart heard in the ear; yet it suggested that to Manuel, and wrought ominously upon his superstition.

He listened. Sudden, soft gust—gentle beat, beat, beat hastening at the end! Was it the wind? How seldom had he heard wind in the jungle! Was it the fronds of the palms or the beating of his heart or of Señor's? His blood did beat thick in his ears. Then a chill passed over him, a certainty of some calamity about to be, beyond his comprehension; and he wrenched decision out of his wavering will, and swore that he would start down the Palcazu on the morrow, if not with this strange companion, then alone.

Manuel fell into a doze. He awakened presently, and sat up, drowsy and hot. He was alone in the shack. Then a hand protruded under the flap of the netting and plucked at him.

"Hurry! Hurry!" came the hoarse whisper. "Don't speak—don't make a noise!"

Wide awake in a second, Manuel swept aside the flap and straightened up outside. Señor stood very close to him. On the instant, low, whirring sounds caught his ear. From the green wall of cane streaked little things that he took for birds. Bright and swift the glints of light shot through the yellow sunshine. All about him they struck with tiny, pattering thuds and spats. Suddenly the shack appeared to be covered with quivering butterflies. They were gaudy, feathered darts from blowguns of the cannibals.

"Cashibos!" yelled Manuel.

"Run! Run!" cried Señor. He thrust his coat over Manuel and turned him with a violent push. "Run for the river!"

The frenzy of his voice and will served almost to make Manuel act automatically. But he looked back, then stood with suspended breath and leaden feet.

Bronze shadows darted through the interstices of the cane. Then the open sunlight burnished small, naked savages, lean, wild, as agile and bounding as if they were made of the rubber of their jungle home.

Señor jerked Manuel's machete from a log of firewood, and rushed to meet them. His back was covered with gaudy butterfly darts. The sight held Manuel stricken in his tracks. Señor had made his broad body a shield, had stood buffer between his comrade and the poisoned darts of the Cashibos.

Like a swarm of copper bees shining in the sun, the cannibals poured out of the cane, incredibly swift and silent, leveling their blowguns and brandishing their spears.

Señor plunged at them, sweeping the machete. A row of nimble bodies wilted before him, went down as grain before a scythe. Again the blade swept backward, to whistle forward and describe a circle through tumbling, copper-colored bodies.

Rooted in horror, Manuel saw the first spear point come out of Señor's back. Another and another! They slipped out as easily as if coming through water. Señor dropped the machete, and swaying, upheld by spears, he broke that silent fight with a terrible cry. It pealed out, piercingly shrill with pain, horrible in its human note of death, but strange and significant in its ringing triumph. Then he fell, and the Cashibos hurdled his body.

Animal instinct to survive burst the bonds that held Manuel as paralyzed. One leap carried him behind the shack, another into the cane, where he sprang into headlong flight. The cane offered little resistance to his giant bounds. Soon he reached the bank of the river. The canoe was gone. Rows of caymans lay along the beach. So swiftly he leaped down that he beat them into the water. Then, drawing Señor's coat tight around his head and shoulders, he plunged out with powerful strokes.

He had gained the middle of the estuary, when he saw arrowy gleams glance before him. Like hissing hail, a shower of darts struck the water. Then it seemed that gaudy butterflies floated about his face. Diving deep, he swam until compelled to rise for breath.

As he came up, a crocodile rolled menacingly near. Manuel hit it a blow with his fist, and dove again. The coat hindered rapid swimming under water. He rose again to hear the crocodile swirling behind him. Darts splashed big drops on his cheeks, tugged at his head covering, streaked beyond him to skitter along the surface of the estuary.

Reaching shallow water, he crawled into the reeds. White-mouthed snakes struck at him. The bank was low and overhung with rank growths. Manuel scrambled through to the solid ground; and then turned to have a look at his pursuers.

Up and down the sandy beach a hundred or more Cashibos were running. How wild they were, how springy and fleet! How similar to the hungry, whirling sand flies! For a moment the disturbed caymans threshed about in the estuary, holding the cannibals back. Presently several of the most daring waded in above the commotion; then others entered below.

Manuel breasted the dense jungle. Before him rose an apparently impenetrable wall of green. He dove into it, tore through it, leaving a trail of broken branches, twisted vines, and turned leaves. In places he ran encumbered by clinging creepers; in others he parted the thick growths with his hands and leaped high to separate them. Again he bent low to crawl along the peccary trails.

Despite the obstacles, he went so swiftly that the jungle pests could not get at him; the few which did could not keep their hold, because of the scraping brush. Soon he ran out of a vine-webbed canebrake into a grove of sitekas, rubber trees, and palms. At every bound he sank into the moist earth, still he kept on running. He heard a scattering of animals before him, and saw a blur of flapping birds.

The day seemed to darken. He looked up to see trees branching at a height of two hundred feet, and intermingling their foliage to obscure sun and sky. Here was the dim shade of the great forest of the Amazon tributaries. Sheering off to the right, he ran until the clinging earth clogged his feet.

The forest was like a huge, dim hall full of humming life. Lines of shrieking monkeys hung on the ropelike vines that reached from the ground to green canopy overhead. Birds of paradise sailed like showers of gold through the thick, hazy air. Before him fled boas, peccaries, ant-eaters, spotted cats, and beasts that he could not name.

Manuel chose the oozy ground, for there the underbrush was not higher than his knees. On and on he wallowed through the moist labyrinth of intricate thickets, of aisles lined by the red capironas, of peccary trails worn in the earth, of glades starry with exquisite orchids. A fragrance of nauseous sweetness, like that of rotting jessamine and tuberose, mingled with fetid odor of wet, hot earth, of ripe life and luxuriance. The forest was steeped in a steam from overheat, overmoisture, overgrowth.

The gloom deepened. Somewhere back of Manuel rasped out the cough of a jaguar. He quickened his weary steps, soon to strike rising ground and pass out of the dark forest into groves of *sitekas*. The day was waning. He ascended a ridge, following the patches of open ground where the baked clay shone white. This hard ground would hide his trail from the cannibals, but he had no hope of eluding the jaguars. Still, he could climb out of reach of the hunting cats. It was the little, winged devils, the tiny, creeping fiends that most menaced his life.

He strode on till the shadows warned him of approaching night. Selecting a group of palms with tops interlocking, he climbed one, and perched in the midst of the stems of the leaves. Laboriously he broke stem after stem, bent and laid them crosswise in the middle of the tree. Then he straddled another stem, let his feet hang down, and lay back upon the rude floor he had constructed. Finally, wrapping head and face in Señor's coat and hiding his hands, he composed himself to rest.

He was dripping wet, hot as fire, pulsating, seething, aching, his whole body inflamed. Gradually the riot of his nerves, the race of hot blood subsided and cooled. Night set in, and the jungle awoke to the hue and cry of its bloody denizens. Mosquitoes swarmed around his perch with a continuous hum not unlike the long, low roll of a drum. Huge bats whizzed to and fro, brushing the palm leaves. Light steps on the hard clay, rustling of brush and snapping of twigs attested to the movement of peccaries. These sounds significantly ceased at the stealthy, padded tread of a jaguar. From distant points came the hungry snarl, the fighting squall, the ominous cough of the jungle cats.

Sometime late in the night Manuel fell asleep. When he awoke the fog clouds were mustering, bulging, mushrooming all in a swirl as they lifted. Like a disk of molten silver, the sun glared through the misty curtain. The drip, drip, drip of dew was all the sound to break the silence. Manuel's cramped muscles made descending to the ground an awkward task.

He estimated that his flight had taken him miles into the interior. Evidently for the time being he had eluded the Cashibos. However, his situation was gravely critical, and he would never be safe until he got clear of Palcazu territory. It was impossible for him to protect himself from the jungle parasites. His instant and inflexible determination was to make his way back to the river, find his canoe, or steal one from the cannibals, and, failing both, lash some logs together and trust to the current.

The rains were due; soon the rivers would be raging floods; he would make fast time. Manuel had no fear of starvation, of the deadly heat, the fatal dews, the rainy-season fever, or of the Cashibos. What he feared was the infernal flies, ticks, ants, mosquitoes—the whole blood-sucking horde. Well he knew that they might bite him blind, poison his blood, drive him mad, actually kill him before he got out of the jungle.

As he was about to start, a small leather pocketbook fell from Señor's coat. Manuel picked it up. He saw again those broad shoulders covered with the gaudy butterfly darts. He drew his breath with a sharp catch. Fingering the little book, unaccountably impelled, he opened it. Inside was a picture.

He looked down into the dark, challenging eyes, the piquant, alluring face of the woman who had been his sweetheart wife!

Manuel smiled dreamily. How clear was the vision! But almost instantly he jerked up his head, hid the picture, and gazed furtively about him, trembling and startled. The glaring jungle was no lying deceit of the fancy.

Slowly he drew forth the picture. Again the proud, dark eyes, the sweet lips, the face arch with girl's willfulness, importunate with woman's charm!

Manuel shifted his straining gaze to Señor's coat.

"Señor! He was the man—that sailor from over the sea—whom she loved at Malaga! What does it all mean? I felt his secret—I lied—I hatched that murderous story to help him. But he knew I did not kill her!"

Manuel pitched high his arms, quivering, riven by the might of the truth.

"He recognized me! He knew me all the time! He saved my life!"

Manuel fell backward and lay motionless, with his hands shutting out the light. An hour passed. At last he arose, half dazed, fighting to understand.

With Señor's coat and the picture before him, he traced the wonderful association between them and him. There were the plain facts, as clear in his sight as the pictured face of the woman who had ruined him, but they were bewildering: he could feel but not comprehend them. They obscured their meaning in mystery, in the inscrutable mystery of human life. He had freed her, had left her to be happy with the man she loved.

Had she betrayed him, too? It was not impossible that a woman who had ceased to love one man would cease to love his successor. Some subtle meaning pervaded the atmosphere of that faded coat, that leather book, that woman's face, with its smile, and by the meaning Manuel knew Señor had suffered the same stunning stroke that had blighted him. Señor had cried out in the night: "Oh God, let me forget!"

It was the same story—hell in the mind, because one day on a woman's face shone that mysterious thing, a light, a smile for him alone, and on the next day it vanished. Fever in the blood, madness to forget, wandering, a hunt for peace, and the wasting years—how he knew them!

Manuel thought of Señor, of his magnificent strength, of the lion in him as he sprang to meet the Cashibos, of the gaudy butterfly darts imbedded in his back, of the glory and pathos of his death. What his life might have been! A strung cord snapped in Manuel's breast; his heart broke. Bitter salt tears flowed for Señor, for himself, for all miserable wretches for all time. In that revealing moment he caught a glimpse of the infinite. He saw the helplessness of man, the unintelligible fatality of chance, motive, power, charm, love—all that made up the complexity of life.

How little it mattered, from the view of what made life significant to him, that he was a rubber hunter, lost in the jungle, hunted by cannibals, tortured by heat, thirst, hunger, vermin! His real life was deep-seated in the richly colored halls of memory; and when he lived at all, it was when he dreamed therein. His outside existence, habits of toil, and debauchery were horrors that he hated. On the outside he was a brutalized rubber hunter, unkempt and unwashed, a coarse clod, given over to gaming and *chicha*. In that inner life he lived on a windy hill, watching white sails on a blue sea, listening to a woman's voice.

But some change had come that would now affect his exterior life; something beautiful crowned the hideous span of years. His companionship with Señor had softened him, and the tragedy, with its divine communication of truth, was a lightning flash into the black gulf of his soul.

By its light he felt pity for her, for Señor, for himself, for all who lived and loved and suffered. By its light he divined the intricate web and tangle and cross and counter-cross of the instincts and feelings of human nature—all that made love transient in one heart, steadfast in another, fleeting as the shadow of a flitting wing—wonderful, terrible, unquenchable as the burning sun.

By its light he saw woman, the mother of life, the source of love, the fountain of joy, the embodiment of change—nature's tool to further her unfathomable design, forever and ever to lure man by grace and beauty, to win him, to fetter him in unattainable, ever-enthralling desires. By its light he saw himself another man, a long-tried, long-failing man, faithful to his better self at the last.

Manuel set forth toward the river, keeping in the shade of trees, walking cautiously, with suspicious eyes ever on the outlook. He walked all day, covering twice the distance he calculated he had fled inland. When night fell, he went on by the light of the stars until the fog obscured them. The rest of the night he walked round a tree with covered head. In the morning the sun rose on the side he had thought was west. He had become lost in the jungle.

Heretofore panic had always seized him on a like occasion; this time it did not. Taking the direction he thought right, he pressed on till the midday sun boiled his blood. Succulent leaves and the pith of small palms served as food.

He moistened his parching mouth with the sap of trees. Lying down, he covered himself with the coat and a pile of brush and slept; then awoke to trudge on, fighting the flies.

He entered the great jungle forest, and sought his back trail, but did not find it. Swampy water allayed his thirst, and a snake served for meat. The jaguars drove him out of the forest. He began to wander in a circle; and that night and the following day and the next were but augmented repetitions of what had gone before.

The rains did not come. The fronds of the palms beat in the still air. Manuel heard in them a knell. Bitten blind, flayed alive by pests, he fell at last with clouded mind. The whizzing wheel of flies circled lower; the armies of marching ants spread over him; the red splotches of ticks on the leaves spilled themselves upon him like quicksilver. He crawled on through the hot bushes. The light of his mind wavered, and he raved of infernal fires. He was rolling in fire; forked tongues of flame licked at his flesh; red sparks ate into his brain. Down, down under the heated earth, through hot vapors blown by fiery gusts! It was a jungle with underbrush of flame, trees in the image of pillars of fire, screeching red monkeys in service as imps, birds of dazzling coals; and over all and under all and through all a vast humming horde of living embers that bit with white-hot teeth.

As Manuel's reason flickered, ready to go out forever, the rain descended, and it cooled him and washed him clean of insects. It slaked his thirst and soothed his blinded eyes. At length the tropical cloudburst roared away, leaving the jungle drenched. Manuel followed a rushing stream of water that he knew would lead him to the river. In him resurged effort and resistance.

By nightfall he had come to the border of cane. Like an eel through grass, he slipped between the stalks to the river. On the opposite shore faint lights twinkled. At first he took them for fireflies. But dark forms moving across the lights told him he had stumbled upon an encampment of the Cashibos.

The river seemed uneasy, stirring. It was rising fast. By dawn it would be bank full with a swift current. Under the pale stars the water shimmered, steely black in the shade of overhanging shore, dead silver in the center, where the fish swirled and the crocodiles trailed dimpling wakes.

Without hesitation, Manuel stepped into the water, noiselessly sinking himself to his neck. With his ear level with the surface, he subordinated every sense to that of hearing. The river was a sounding board, augmenting the faint jungle sounds. Crossing would be as safe for him then as it would ever be.

Grim as death, Manuel trusted himself to the river. He glided off the shoal without making a ripple, and swam deep with guarded strokes. Fish sported before him; spiders and snakes grazed his cheeks; caymans floated by with knotty snout parting the current, and lines of bubbles bursting with hollow sound betrayed the underwater passage of more of the lazy reptiles.

Once Manuel felt the swirl and heave of water disturbed by a powerful force. A soft river breeze wafted to him the smell of burning wood and the dull roar of distant rapids. He crossed the shimmering space between the shadows of shore. Looking backward, he descried a circle of black snouts lazily closing in upon him. He quickened his strokes. The twinkling lights disappeared. All before him was black. He felt slimy reeds touch his face, and, lowering his feet, found the bottom, and cautiously waded out. Then he crouched down to rest to gather all his wit and strength for the final move.

Toward the bank he could not see his hand before his face; riverward there was a glancing sheen of water that made the gloom opaque. He began to crawl, feeling in the darkness for a canoe. Moving downstream, he worked out of the marshy sedge to ground worn smooth and hard. It was a landing place for canoes.

He strained his eyes. All about him were shadowy, merging shades without shape. The low murmur of strange voices halted him; he was within hearing of the cannibals. Then in him awoke the stealth and savage spirit of a jaguar stalking prey. Gliding up the trail, he peeped over the bank. Fires flickered back in the blackness, lighting wan circles that were streaked and shadowed by moving, dark forms. With fateful eyes Manuel watched.

Below him a slight splash drew his attention. He fancied it too thin, too hard and dead, to be made by water creature. Again it broke the silence, unnatural to his trained ear. It was the splash of a paddle. Soundless as the shadows about him, Manuel glided down to the edge of the river and lay flat, hugging the sand.

A long, low canoe, black against the background of the river gloom, swept in to the landing gloom, swept in to the landing, grated on the sand, and spread gentle, lapping waves against the beach. A slender form, smooth and wild in outline, stepped out within a yard of Manuel.

Like a specter Manuel loomed up, and his hands closed vise-tight around the neck of the cannibal. He lifted him clear of the ground, and there held him, wrestling, wriggling till fierce struggles ceased in spasmodic convulsions and these subsided in a slow, trembling stretch.

When the body hung limp, Manuel laid it down, and looked up the dim trail leading to the camp of the Cashibos. Upon him was the spell to kill. He saw again the gaudy butterfly darts in Señor's back; he heard again that strange, terrible cry of triumph. Over him surged Señor's grand disdain of life. Almost he yielded to an irresistible impulse to make that the end.

"If I had my machete—" he thought. Then he threw off the insidious thrall, and, stepping into the canoe, picked up the paddle and pushed out into the river. The twinkling lights vanished in the foliage. There was no sound of pursuit; the dreamy jungle hum remained unbroken. He paddled the light canoe swiftly with the current.

The moon rose, whitening the river lane. A breeze bore the boom of the Palcazu in flood. Once upon that river of rapids, Manuel would scorn pursuit. Slackening current told him that backwater had swelled the estuary. Soon his ears filled with the rumbling of waters, and he turned out of the estuary into the sliding, moon-blanched Palcazu.

As he dipped into the glistening channel of the first rapid, the canoe, quivering and vibrating, seemed to lurch into the air. Shock on shock kept the bow leaping. Manuel crouched low in the stern. It took all the strength of his brawny arms to keep the canoe straight. Whirling suck holes raced with him; frothy waves curled along the gunwales. One rapid led into another, until the Palcazu was a thundering succession of broken waters. It ran wild for freedom. In the plunging inclines, the silver-crested channels, the bulging billows, were the hurry and spirit of the river. The current, splitting on blackheaded stones, hissed its hatred of restraint. Manuel guided the canoe from side to side, glancing along the gulfs, fringing the falls, always abreast of the widest passages.

A haze crept over the moon and thickened to gray fog. Shadows shrouded the river, hanging lower and lower, descending to mingle with the spray. Manuel paddled on while the hours passed.

The fog curtain lightened to the coming of dawn. Manuel evinced no surprise to find himself gazing upon the misty flood of the wide Pachitea. He had run the Palcazu in one night. Paddling ashore, he beached the canoe to bail out water he had shipped in that wild ride.

All night he had felt a balancing of some kind of cargo in the bow. Upon investigating, he found the bottom of the bow covered with palm leaves. These he lifted to discover two naked little savages cowering on a mat of woven reeds.

"Cashibos!" ejaculated Manuel. "Boy and girl. They were in the canoe last night when I strangled that fellow, their father, probably. What's to be done with them?"

The boy was a dark copper color; his hair grew straight down over his low forehead; he was pot-bellied and altogether ugly. The girl was younger, lighter in color, slim and graceful, and pretty in a wild way, like a bronze elf of the jungle.

"What'll I do with them?" repeated Manuel. "I can't kill them, or leave them here to starve or be eaten by jaguars. I'll take them down the Pachitea and turn them over to a Campas tribe."

Having decided, Manuel folded a palm leaf and used it to bail out the canoe. In the bottom he found a bunch of dwarfish bananas and some dried fish. Here was good fortune in the way of food. He arranged the palm leaves across the gunwales, making a sun, rain, and dew shield. Then, pushing off, he paddled into the swollen current.

The blazing sun rose; the sand flies wheeled with the drifting canoe; the afternoon rain poured; night came, with its cloud of singing mosquitoes, its poison dews and fogs.

That day passed, and another like it. Every hour the canoe drifted speedy as the current. The Cashibos children lost their fear of Manuel. The boy jabbered and played; the girl smiled at Manuel, which persuaded him not to give them to a Campas tribe, but to take them home and care for them himself.

Three more days and nights the canoe drifted. Manuel's strength had returned, but it troubled him to think. Something had happened up the river. He had for his pillow a ragged coat that fascinated him, and which he treasured.

Early the next morning he turned the green bend at La Boca to come abruptly upon the *Amazonas*, lying at the dock. Men shouted from her decks; there was a thudding of bare feet.

"Look! Look!"

"Is it the outlaw?"

"No—no!"

"Yes—yes. Those shoulders and arms—it's he!"

Manuel's blotched face, swollen out of all proportions, was unrecognizable.

Captain Valdez leaned hard over the rail. "Manuel, is it you?"

"Yes, captain."

"Where's your cowcha?"

"Lost, captain, lost! A great rubber forest, captain—I had tons of cowcha—it's lost—all lost!"

"I suppose so," replied Valdez ironically. "That's a fine cargo to pay you—two half-grown Indian kids. The nerve of you, Manuel, dropping into La Boca with slaves."

"Slaves!" echoed from Manuel. His gaze traveled from Valdez's face to the little bronze Cashibos, once more huddling, frightened, in the bow. "Slaves? Ha! Ha! Ha!"

"Manuel, you had your choice," went on the captain, "and now you must abide by it. I've caught some of you slave hunters this trip. There's Bustos in irons. Your choice Manuel—the chain gang, or the river?"

"The river for me!" said Manuel. "Only up instead of down!"

"Up! But, Manuel, there's a chance down the Amazon. You—"

The rubber hunter faced up the wide Pachitea. His stentorian cry froze the words upon Captain Valdez's lips. It rolled out, a strange, trenchant call to something beyond the wild, silent river.

"Fever," whispered one of the fettered slave dealers.

"Bitten crazy," said another.

Manuel started the canoe upstream. He did not look back.

Captain and crew and prisoners on the boat thrilled to Bustos's mocking farewell.

"*Adios*, Manuel!"

THE END

FOOTNOTE

[1] Recently the Mexican government changed its policy toward peon labor in Yucatan, and the Yaquis in Sonora. These Indians are now in the regular Mexican army. [AUTHOR'S NOTE.]

Booksophile
Your Local Online Bookstore

Buy Books Online from

www.Booksophile.com

Explore our collection of books written in various languages and uncommon topics from different parts of the world, including history, art and culture, poems, autobiography and bibliographies, cooking, action & adventure, world war, fiction, science, and law.

Add to your bookshelf or gift to another lover of books - first editions of some of the most celebrated books ever published. From classic literature to bestsellers, you will find many first editions that were presumed to be out-of-print.

Free shipping globally for orders worth US$ 100.00.

Use code "Shop_10" to avail additional 10% on first order.

Visit today
www.booksophile.com

Milton Keynes UK
Ingram Content Group UK Ltd.
UKHW011104201123
432908UK00007B/1341

9 789357 922548